MW01630337

1972

WHAT A YEAR IT WAS!

A walk back in time...

To

From

FLICKBACK

Managing Editor/Publisher • Art Worthington
Design, Writing & Research • Peter Hess

www.FLICKBACK.com
(800) 541-3533

Contents

JOHN
LENNON
ONE TO ONE
MADISON SQUARE GARDEN
Arts
&
Entertainment

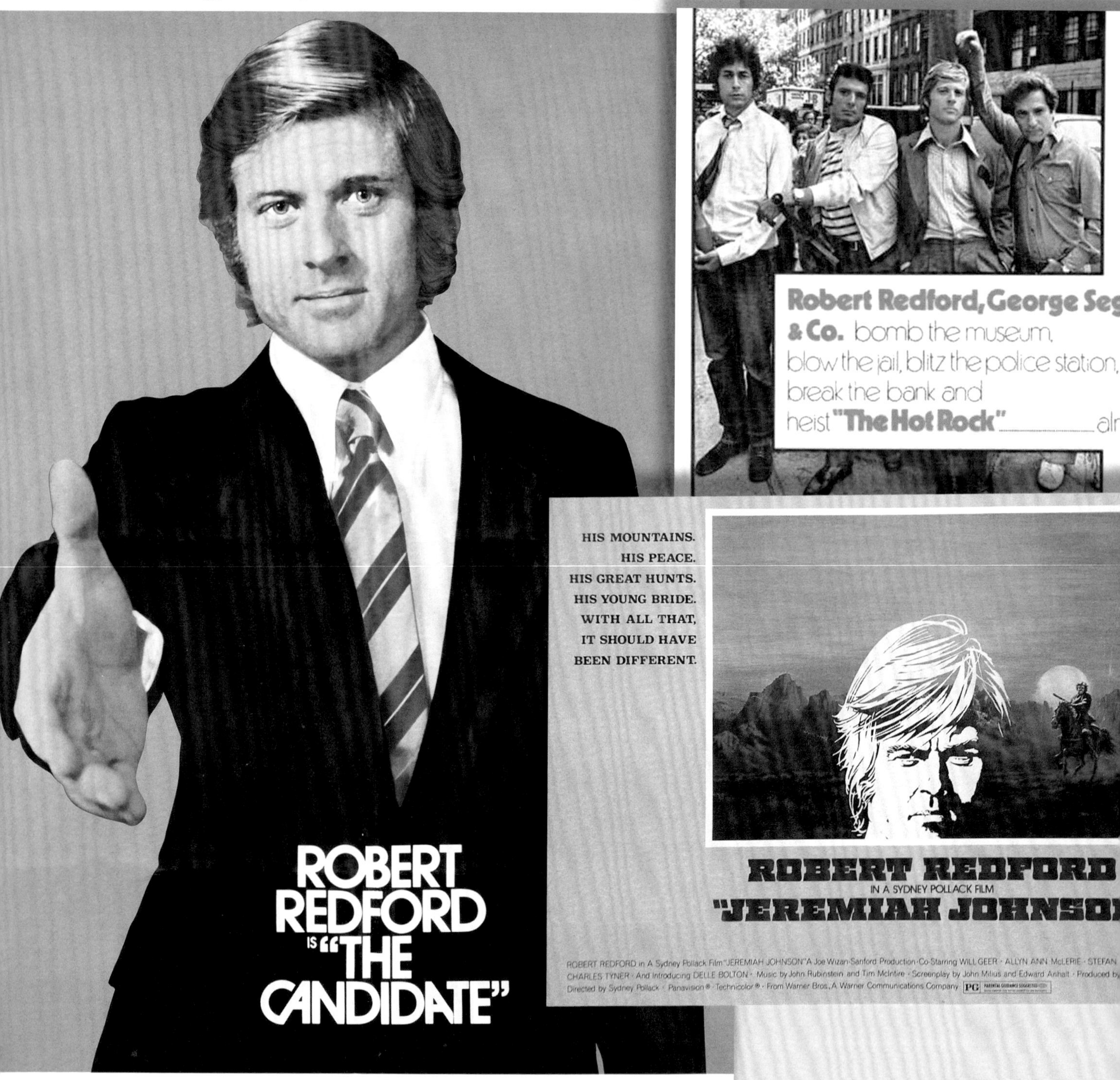

After a year off and two years after his success in the smash-hit western *Butch Cassidy and the Sundance Kid*, which paired him with **Paul Newman**, lavishly handsome movie star **Robert Redford** finds the spotlight again with a trio of new films. He returns to the western format with *Jeremiah Johnson*, playing an isolated mountain trapper whose adversarial relationship with Native Americans gradually gives way to mutual respect.

Jeremiah Johnson proves to be one of the year's top box office hits. Next, he stars as California senatorial hopeful Bill McCay in the satirical political drama, *The Candidate*. The film garners good reviews and a Best Writing Oscar, though it doesn't make *Jeremiah Johnson* money. Redford wraps up the year with the crime caper comedy *The Hot Rock* which, unfortunately, is cooly greeted by critics and filmgoers alike.

Movies
CELLULOID
Standouts

Director **Francis Ford Coppola's** crime family drama, *The Godfather*, is perhaps the most consequential and profitable film to grace screens in 1972. Based on a **Mario Puzo** novel, **Marlon Brando** stars as the mumbling Mafia patriarch presiding over a squabbling clan while the unlikely youngest son (**Al Pacino**) slowly asserts himself as the future Don. The first installment in an influential trilogy chronicling the ruthless Corleone family, the movie features **James Caan**, **Robert Duvall** and **Diane Keaton**.

The tense thriller *Deliverance* follows four businessmen on a canoe holiday in the remote Southern outback, where they become the brutalized victims of creepy mountain men. **Burt Reynolds**, **Jon Voight** & **Ned Beatty** head the cast.

A pair of musical movies with strong female leads are standouts. Supremes singer **Diana Ross** undertakes the role of the great jazz vocalist, Billie Holliday in *Lady Sings the Blues*. The biopic paints a portrait of Lady Day's harrowing struggles with poverty, drug addiction, racism and prison, culminating in her Carnegie Hall triumph. **Billy Dee Williams** and **Richard Pryor** co-star.

Cabaret is one of the best musicals ever, first on the Broadway stage and then triumphantly brought to film. All of the songs are good, and **Liza Minelli** as American Sally Bowles performing in a decadent 1931 Berlin nightclub is incandescent. Minelli wins the Best Actress Oscar, **Joel Grey** takes Best Supporting Actor and **Bob Fosse** is Best Director.

From today's perspective, perhaps **Woody Allen** isn't the first person you would approach to learn *Everything You Always Wanted to Know About Sex But Were Afraid to Ask*, but the 1972 comedy is a big hit for the writer/director/actor, as is *Play it Again, Sam*, wherein he portrays a film critic coached in dating by the ghost of Humphrey Bogart.

Diana Ross in Lady Sings the Blues

Jerry Lacy & Woody Allen in Play it Again, Sam

Marlon Brando as Don Vito Corleone in The Godfather

Bluebeard
BOXCAR BERTHA
Brother Sun, Sister Moon
Buck and the Preacher
BUTTERFLIES ARE FREE
The Canterbury Tales
CHATO'S LAND
CHILD'S PLAY
CISCO PIKE
Come Back, Charleston Blue
THE COWBOYS
The Effect of Gamma Rays on Man-in-the-Moon Marigolds
Fat City
FRENZY
FRITZ THE CAT
Fuzz
THE GETAWAY
The Great Northfield Minnesota Raid
HAMMERSMITH IS OUT
The Heartbreak Kid
HIT MAN

1776
ACROSS 110TH STREET
The Anderson Tapes
Antony and Cleopatra
The Assassination of Trotsky
Avanti!
BAD COMPANY

JOE KIDD
Junior Bonner
Kansas City Bomber
The Life and Times of Judge Roy Bean
The MECHANIC
The NEW CENTURIONS
THE OFFENCE
Pancho Villa
Pete 'n' Tillie
The Poseidon Adventure
PRIME CUT
The Ruling Class
SAVAGE MESSIAH
SILENT RUNNING
SKYJACKED
Slaughterhouse-Five
SLEUTH
SOUNDER
State of Siege
They Only Kill Their Masters
Travels with My Aunt
UNDER MILKWOOD
The Valachi Papers
The War Between Men and Women
What's Up, Doc?
WHERE DOES IT HURT?

The Academy Awards

"And The Winner Is..."

Oscars® Presented in 1972 *(for 1971 Films)*

BEST PICTURE
THE FRENCH CONNECTION

BEST ACTOR
GENE HACKMAN,
The French Connection

BEST ACTRESS
JANE FONDA,
Klute

BEST DIRECTOR
WILLIAM FRIEDKIN,
The French Connection

BEST SUPPORTING ACTOR
BEN JOHNSON, *The Last Picture Show*

BEST SUPPORTING ACTRESS
CLORIS LEACHMAN, *The Last Picture Show*

BEST SONG
"THEME FROM SHAFT," *Shaft* (by Isaac Hayes)

Jane Fonda

1972 Favorites *(Oscars® Presented in 1973)*

BEST PICTURE
THE GODFATHER

BEST ACTOR
MARLON BRANDO,
The Godfather

BEST ACTRESS
LIZA MINELLI,
Cabaret

BEST DIRECTOR
BOB FOSSE, *Cabaret*

BEST SUPPORTING ACTOR
JOEL GREY, *Cabaret*

BEST SUPPORTING ACTRESS
EILEEN HECKART, *Butterflies Are Free*

BEST SONG
"THE MORNING AFTER,"
The Poseidon Adventure

Joel Grey

44th Annual Academy Awards Ceremony

• April 10, 1972 •
Dorothy Chandler Pavilion

On the Red Carpet...

Screen legend Helen Hayes

Oscar-winning composer Isaac Hayes & his Grandma

Sammy Davis, Jr. serves as Oscar host, along with **Helen Hayes**, **Alan King** & **Jack Lemmon**.

Gene Hackman, from top, **Janc Fonda**, and presenters **Liza Minelli**, **Walter Matthau** and **Jack Nicholson**.

Charlie Chaplin receives an honorary Oscar from **Jack Lemmon**.

Raquel Welch poses with Oscar winners **Cloris Leachman** and **Gene Hackman**.

The 30th GOLDEN GLOBE AWARDS

Honoring the best in film and television for 1972 and bestowed on January 28, 1973 by members of the Hollywood Foreign Press Association

BEST MOTION PICTURE - Drama
The Godfather

Comedy or Musical
Cabaret

BEST ACTOR - Drama
Marlon Brando
The Godfather

BEST ACTRESS - Drama
Liv Ullmann
The Emigrants

BEST ACTOR - Comedy/Musical
Jack Lemmon
Avanti

BEST ACTRESS - Comedy/Musical
Liza Minelli
Cabaret

BEST SUPPORTING ACTOR
Joel Grey
Cabaret

BEST SUPPORTING ACTRESS
Shelley Winters
The Poseidon Adventure

BEST DIRECTOR
Francis Ford Coppola
The Godfather

RATED X? COME ON IN!

An 'X' rating is designed to serve as a caution to audiences that a film may contain prurient material. But for some, it is an enticing lure.

Marlon Brando portrays a widowed American who begins an anonymous sexual relationship with a Parisian woman in Italian director **Bernardo Bertolucci's** *Last Tango in Paris*, proving that art and eroticism can coexist.

Billed as "an exercise in poor taste," **John Waters'** *Pink Flamingos* goes to any lengths to shock and, frequently, amuse. For those who want the real deal, *Deep Throat* starring **Linda Lovelace** raises the quality bar on pornography just enough to attract a surprisingly large audience of filmgoers. And finally, exactly what we needed, an X-rated feature-length animated comedy: *Fritz the Cat*, created by **Ralph Bakshi**.

Klaus Kinski in Aguirre, the Wrath of God.

1972 **is a fruitful year for international cinema,** with a number of extraordinarily influential foreign films leaving enduring legacies.

From German director/writer/producer **Werner Herzog** comes *Aguirre, the Wrath of God*. **Klaus Kinski** gives an intense performance as a deranged Spaniard leading a group of conquistadors on a doomed expedition down the Amazon. Many critics declare it a masterpiece.

Highly regarded Swedish auteur **Ingmar Bergman** creates *Cries and Whispers*, a distinctly personal telling centered on a family dealing with a sister's terminal cancer diagnosis. The film garners five Academy Award nominations.

A strange dinner party with extraordinary guests comprises the action in *The Discreet Charm of the Bourgeoisie*, a French film directed by surrealist **Luis Buñuel**.

And, *Roma* is an episodic love letter to the city by fabled Italian director **Federico Fellini**, based on his own relocation to Rome as a young man.

The 25th Annual Cannes Film Festival takes place in May 1972. **L'aventure, c'est l'aventure** *by French director* **Claude Lelouche** *opens the festival, while* **Alfred Hitchcock's** *Frenzy is the closer. British director* **Joseph Losey** *heads the jury.*

Roman Polanski, Francesca Annis *&* **Jon Finch** *representing director Polanski's film,* **Macbeth**.

Grand Prix du Festival International du Film
The Working Class Goes to Heaven
by Elio Petri

Grand Prix Spécial du Jury
Solaris
by Andrei Tarkovsky

Best Actress
Susannah York
Images

Best Actor
Jean Yanne
We Won't Grow Old Together

BRUCE LEE may be the most influential martial artist of all time. His Hong Kong and Hollywood-produced films elevate the traditional fight film to new heights of popularity and ignite a surge of interest in the martial arts. His blockbuster early '70s films include *The Big Boss*, *Fist of Fury*, *Way of the Dragon* (directed and written by Lee) and *Enter the Dragon*.

Tragically, Lee would die in 1973, at the age of 32 from diagnosed cerebral edema. *Game of Death* remains an unfinished film project, later released in a couple of different "mashup" versions.

Horror & SCI-FI

Ben

Conquest of the **Planet** of the **Apes**

Dear Dead Delilah

Dr. Phibes Rises Again

Dracula AD 1972

Fear in the **Night**

Godzilla vs. Gigan

I Dismember Mama

The Last House on the **Left**

The Other

The Possession of Joel Delaney

Sisters

Tales from the **Crypt**

The Thing with Two Heads

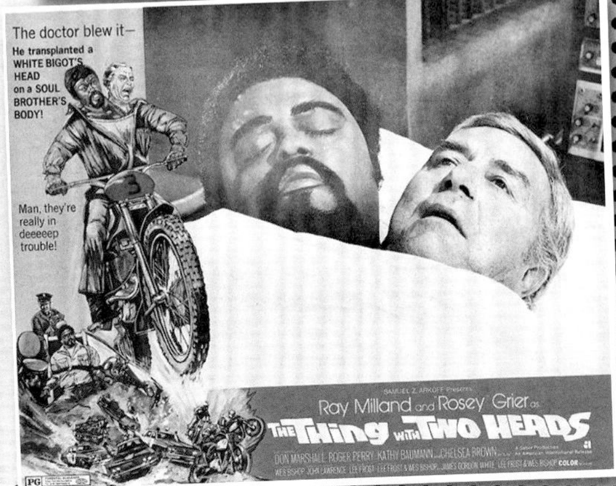

Memorable Lines

THE GODFATHER

Michael: *My father is no different than any powerful man, any man with power, like a president or senator.*
Kay Adams: *Do you know how naive you sound, Michael? Presidents and senators don't have men killed.*
Michael: *Oh. Who's being naive, Kay?*

Peter Clemenza: *Leave the gun. Take the cannoli.*

BUTTERFLIES *are* FREE

Mrs. Baker: *I do not intend to pay money to see nudity, obscenity and degeneracy.*
Ralph: *Mrs. Baker, these things are all a part of life.*
Mrs. Baker: *I know, Mr. Santori. So is diarrhea, but I wouldn't classify it as entertainment.*

Jill: *My mother wanted me to go to UCLA, but I couldn't find a place to park.*

CABARET

Master of Ceremonies: *Outside it is windy, but inside it is so hot, every night we have the battle to keep the girls from taking off all their clothing. So don't go away, who knows? Tonight we may lose the battle!*

Liza Minelli

What's Up, Doc?

Judy: *Love means never having to say you're sorry.*
Howard: *That's the dumbest thing I ever heard.*

Howard: *What are you doing? This is a one way street!*
Judy: *We're only going one way.*

Judy: *Has anyone ever told you that you are very, very sexy?*
Hugh: *Well, actually no.*
Judy: *They never will.*

The TOP-GROSSING 1972 Movies

1. *The Godfather*
2. *The Poseidon Adventure*
3. *What's Up, Doc?*
4. *Deliverance*
5. *Jeremiah Johnson*
6. *Cabaret*
7. *Deep Throat*
8. *The Getaway*
9. *Lady Sings the Blues*
10. *Everything You Always Wanted to Know About Sex*

Steve McQueen, Ali Macgraw in The Getaway

PROGRESS, EXPLOITATION OR BOTH?

An explosion of so-called "**BLAXPLOITATION**" movies proves a popular draw for '70s audiences, but they create a cause for concern among some. On the upside, they provide opportunities for featuring African Americans in leading

film roles. At the same time, they raise questions about the continuing negative depiction of stereotyped Black characters in popular culture.

BLAXPLOITATION 1972

Black Gunn

Black Mama, White Mama

Blacula

Cool Breeze

Hammer

Hit Man

The Legend of N***** Charley

Shaft's Big Score

Slaughter

Super Fly

Trouble Man

PASSINGS

MAURICE CHEVALIER, 83 ACTOR, SINGER ★
WALTER WINCHELL, 74 COMMENTATOR ★
J. ARTHUR RANK, 83 STUDIO EXECUTIVE ★
BRIAN DONLEVY, 71 ACTOR ★ GEORGE
SANDERS, 65 ACTOR ★ MARGARET
RUTHERFORD, 80 ACTRESS ★ OSCAR
LEVANT, 65 ACTOR, PIANIST ★ MAX
FLEISCHER, 89 ANIMATOR ★ MIRIAM HOPKINS,
69 ACTRESS ★ LEO G. CARROLL, 85 ACTOR ★
LOUELLA PARSONS, 91 COLUMNIST

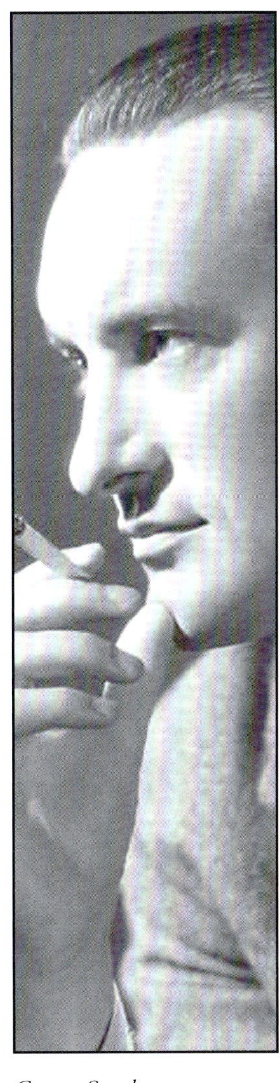
George Sanders

BORN IN 1972

Idris Elba

BEN AFFLECK ★
ELIZABETH BERKLEY ★
CAMERON DIAZ ★
IDRIS ELBA ★ JENNIFER
GARNER ★ DWAYNE
JOHNSON ★ JUDE LAW ★
THANDIE NEWTON ★ GWYNETH
PALTROW ★ AMANDA PEET ★
REBECCA ROMIJN

THE TOP BOX OFFICE
STARS

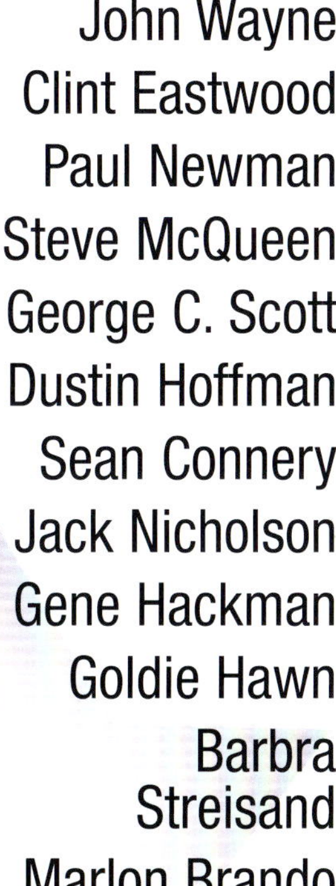
Dustin Hoffman

Gene Hackman

John Wayne
Clint Eastwood
Paul Newman
Steve McQueen
George C. Scott
Dustin Hoffman
Sean Connery
Jack Nicholson
Gene Hackman
Goldie Hawn
Barbra Streisand
Marlon Brando

MOVIE
DEBUTS

Anne Archer
Robert Carradine
Blythe Danner
Jodie Foster
Bob Hoskins
Samuel L. Jackson
Ben Kingsley
John Lithgow
Steve Martin
Nick Nolte
Lily Tomlin
James Woods

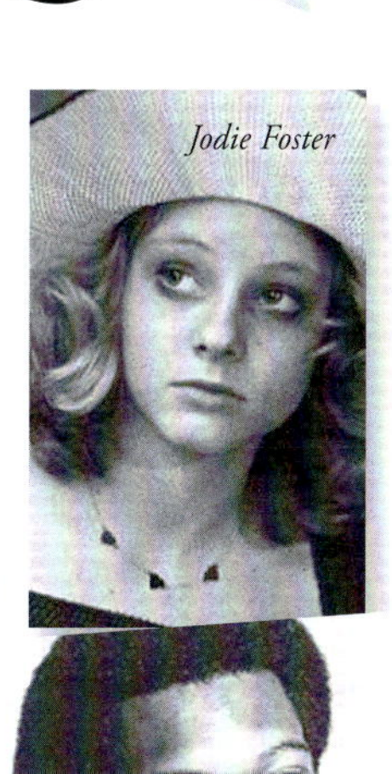
Jodie Foster

Samuel L. Jackson

Kodak

The little camera that
takes big pictures.

It's the new Kodak pocket Instamatic
camera, the one that takes big pictures.
It takes good, clear 3½ x 4½-inch
snapshots. It uses a remarkable new
Kodak color film and has a multi-element
lens. Just drop the new little film cartridge
in the Pocket, and shoot.
Five Pockets to look into. All but one
with automatic exposure control. At your
photo dealer's, from less than $28.
Price subject to change without notice

New Kodak
pocket Instamatic
camera

Actual picture size.

Television

"Great little war we have here"

One of the most beloved and, at 11-seasons, longest-running sitcoms ever, *M*A*S*H* debuts on CBS-TV. Spinning off from the 1970 **Robert Altman** film of the same name, the characters are a team of doctors and staff stationed at a Mobile Army Surgical Hospital (MASH) during the Korean War. Often featuring dark undercurrents, the **Larry Gelbart**-produced series stars **Alan Alda** as sarcastic surgeon "Hawkeye" Pierce and **Loretta Switt** as combative head nurse "Hotlips" Hoolihan. **Jamie Farr**, **Wayne Rogers**, **Harry Morgan**, **Gary Burhoff** and **MacLean Stevenson** round out the nimble cast.

From left: Larry Linville, Loretta Swit, Wayne Rogers, Alan Alda, Gary Burghoff, McLean Stevenson

LONG-RUNNING SITCOMS PREMIERE

Edgy nightclub comic **Redd Foxx** stars as Watts junk dealer Fred Sanford in *SANFORD AND SON* on NBC. **Demond Wilson** plays his long-suffering son, Lamont.

Redd Foxx & Demond Wilson

Outspoken Maude Findley is a sometimes overbearing, die-hard liberal. **Bea Arthur** plays *MAUDE* on CBS and **Bill Macy** is her appliance store owner husband.

Bea Arthur

Comedian **Bob Newhart** portrays a Chicago psychologist in CBS' *THE BOB NEWHART SHOW.* **Suzanne Pleshette** is in the role of his supportive wife.

Bob Newhart & Suzanne Pleshette

Cast of The Waltons

NEW SHOWS
ON THE TV BLOCK

The Waltons

Kung Fu

Emergency!

The Streets of San Francisco

The Rookies

Great Performances on PBS

The Price is Right debuts in a new format on CBS with **Bob Barker** hosting. It is one of the longest-running shows in TV history.

— SHOWS LEAVING THE AIR —

- *The Courtship of Eddie's Father* (1969-1972)
- *My Three Sons* (1960-1972)
- *Bewitched* (1964-1972)
- *The Road Runner Show* (1966-1972)

Julie Andrews

Although ***The Julie Andrews Hour*** is cancelled after a single season, the ABC variety show is a critical favorite and winner of seven Emmy Awards out of ten nominations.

1972 PRIMETIME LINEUP

		7:00	7:30	8:00	8:30	9:00	9:30	10:00	10:30
SATURDAY	ABC	Local		Alias Smith and Jones/Kung Fu		The Streets of San Francisco		The Sixth Sense	
	CBS	Local		All in the Family	Bridget Loves Bernie	Mary Tyler Moore Show	The Bob Newhart Show	Mission: Impossible	
	NBC	Local		Emergency!		NBC Saturday Night at the Movies			
SUNDAY	ABC	Local		The F.B.I.		The ABC Sunday Night Movie			
	CBS	Local	Anna and the King	M*A*S*H	Mannix		Barnaby Jones		Local
	NBC	Wild Kingdom	The Wonderful World of Disney	The NBC Sunday Mystery Movie (Columbo/McCloud/McMillan & Wife			Night Gallery		Local
MONDAY	ABC	Local		The Rookies		Monday Night Football			
	CBS	Local		Gunsmoke		Here's Lucy	Doris Day Show	The New Bill Cosby Show	
	NBC	Local		Rowan & Martin's Laugh-In		NBC Monday Night at the Movies			
TUESDAY	ABC	Local		Temperatures Rising	ABC Tuesday Movie of the Week			Marcus Welby, MD	
	CBS	Local		Maude	Hawaii Five-O		The New CBS Tuesday Night Movies		
	NBC	Local		Bonanza		The Bold Ones: The New Doctors		NBC Reports	
WEDNESDAY	ABC	Local		The Paul Lynde Show	ABC Wednesday Movie of the Week		Owen Marshall, Counselor at Law		
	CBS	Local		The Carol Burnett Show		Medical Center		Cannon	
	NBC	Local		Adam-12	NBC Wednesday Mystery Movie: Madigan/Cool Million/Banacek			Search	
THURSDAY	ABC	Local		The Mod Squad		The Men: Assignment Vienna/Delphi Bureau		The Streets of San Francisco	
	CBS	Local		The Waltons		The CBS Thursday Night Movie			
	NBC	Local		The Flip Wilson Show		Ironside		The Dean Martin Show	
FRIDAY	ABC	Local		The Brady Bunch	Partridge Family	Room 222	The Odd Couple	Love American Style	
	CBS	Local		Sonny & Cher Comedy Hour		The CBS Friday Night Movies			
	NBC	Local		Sanford & Son	Ghost Story		Banyon		

- John Lennon and Yoko Ono are co-hosts for a week on *The Mike Douglas Show.*

- *The Tonight Show Starring Johnny Carson* relocates from New York City to the NBC studios in Burbank, California.

- *Dick Clark's New Year's Rockin' Eve* airs for the first time.

Lennon & Ono

NEW CARTOONS

- ✹ Fat Albert and the Cosby Kids
- ✰ The New Scooby-Doo Movies
- ✹ The Brady Kids
- ✰ The Flintstone Comedy Hour
- ✹ Josie and the Pussycats in Outer Space

Josie and the Pussycats in Outer Space

Best Dramatic Series
Elizabeth R

Best Comedy Series
All in the Family

Best Variety Series
The Carol Burnett Show

Best Drama Series Actor
Peter Falk *Columbo*

Best Drama Series Actress
Glenda Jackson *Elizabeth R*

Best Comedy Series Actor
Carrol O'Connor *All in the Family*

Best Comedy Series Actress
Jean Stapleton
All in the Family

Cast of All in the Family: *Carrol O'Connor, Jean Stapleton, Rob Reiner, Sally Struthers*

BORN IN 1972

SELMA BLAIR ★ WAYNE BRADY ★ NICOLE EGGERT ★ JENNIE GARTH ★ ALYSSA MILANO ★ TRACEE ELLIS ROSS ★ MAYA RUDOLPH ★ CHUCK TODD ★ SOFÍA VERGARA ★ MARLON WAYANS

Sofía Vergara

DIED IN 1972

DAN BLOCKER, 43 BONANZA ACTOR ★ LEO G. CARROLL, 85 BRITISH ACTOR

Dan Blocker

LOS ANGELES' FAVORITE ALBUMS

Last Week	This Week	Title	Artist	Weeks
(2)	1.	HARVEST	Neil Young	6
(1)	2.	AMERICA	America	7
(3)	3.	MALO	Malo	10
(9)	4.	FRAGILE	Yes	7
(6)	5.	PAUL SIMON	Paul Simon	9
(4)	6.	NILSSON SCHMILSSON	Nilsson	8
(8)	7.	CAROLE KING MUSIC	Carole King	18
(7)	8.	AMERICAN PIE	Don McLean	18
(5)	9.	BABY I'M-A WANT YOU	Bread	9
(10)	10.	ELECTRIC WARRIOR	T. Rex	10
(16)	11.	TAPESTRY	Carole King	51
(13)	12.	YOUNG, GIFTED AND BLACK	Aretha Franklin	5
(11)	13.	L.A. MIDNIGHT	B. B. King	7
(19)	14.	WHATCHA SEE IS WHATCHA GET	The Dramatics	3
(—)	15.	FIRST TAKE	Roberta Flack	1
(14)	16.	MADMAN ACROSS THE WATER	Elton John	20
(18)	17.	IN THE WEST	Jimi Hendrix	6
(12)	18.	THE CONCERT FOR BANGLA DESH	Various Artists	15
(20)	19.	TEASER AND THE FIRECAT	Cat Stevens	28
(23)	20.	THE NEW SANTANA ALBUM	Santana	25
(28)	21.	SOLID ROCK	The Temptations	4
(22)	22.	EAT A PEACH	Allman Brothers	2
(27)	23.	LET'S STAY TOGETHER	Al Green	4
(15)	24.	CHEECH & CHONG	Cheech & Chong	22
(—)	25.	STYLISTICS	The Stylistics	1
(—)	26.	ALL DAY MUSIC	War	1
(—)	27.	SMOKIN'	Humble Pie	1
(21)	28.	HOT ROCKS	Rolling Stones	13
(—)	29.	INDIVIDUALLY & COLLECTIVELY	The 5th Dimension	1
(—)	30.	BOBBY WHITLOCK	Bobby Whitlock	1

NEW MUSIC

Title	Artist
I SAW THE LIGHT	Todd Rundgren
DO YOUR THING	Isaac Hayes
EVERY DAY OF MY LIFE	Bobby Vinton

KHJ NEWS!

be an earwitness with . . .

J. PAUL HUDDLESTON

LYLE KILGORE

MARV HOWARD

BOB LEE

JOHN FERRIS

BILL BROWN

CHRIS AMES

HOWARD KING

DONOVAN GATUS

93/KHJ "THIRTY"

MARCH 28, 1972

Last Week	This Week	Title	Artist	Weeks
(3)	1.	A HORSE WITH NO NAME	America	6
(2)	2.	SUAVECITO	Malo	7
(5)	3.	PUPPY LOVE	Donny Osmond	4
(8)	4.	I GOTCHA	Joe Tex	5
(1)	5.	HEART OF GOLD	Neil Young	9
(14)	6.	IN THE RAIN	The Dramatics	4
(9)	7.	DON'T SAY YOU DON'T REMEMBER	Beverly Bremers	5
(4)	8.	WITHOUT YOU	Nilsson	13
(13)	9.	A COWBOYS WORK IS NEVER DONE	Sonny & Cher	5
(6)	10.	BANG A GONG (Get It On)	T. Rex	8
(16)	11.	TAURUS	Dennis Coffey & The Detroit Guitar Band	3
(24)	12.	THE FIRST TIME EVER I SAW YOUR FACE	Roberta Flack	2
(23)	13.	BETCHA BY GOLLY, WOW	The Stylistics	3
(10)	14.	LOUISIANNA	Mike Kennedy	9
(7)	15.	THE WAY OF LOVE	Cher	10
(20)	16.	THE FAMILY OF MAN	Three Dog Night	3
(19)	17.	ROUNDABOUT	Yes	4
(12)	18.	EVERYTHING I OWN	Bread	10
(21)	19.	ROCK AND ROLL LULLABY	B. J. Thomas	6
(22)	20.	TAKE A LOOK AROUND	The Temptations	4
(11)	21.	MOTHER AND CHILD REUNION	Paul Simon	8
(25)	22.	VINCENT	Don McLean	3
(27)	23.	I DIDN'T GET TO SLEEP AT ALL	The 5th Dimension	2
(26)	24.	MISTER CAN'T YOU SEE	Buffy Sainte-Marie	3
(28)	25.	DAY DREAMING	Aretha Franklin	2
(30)	26.	BACK OFF BOOGALOO	Ringo Starr	2
(—)	27.	ROCKIN' ROBIN	Michael Jackson	1
(—)	28.	I'M MOVIN' ON	John Kay	1

© Sony Corp. of America. Visit our Showroom, 714 Fifth Ave. New York, N.Y.

Take-along Stereo.

You don't have to settle for monaural any more when you go to the beach or the park or on a picnic.

Just take along a Sony MR-9300WA.

It's a portable stereo radio that's as easy to take along as any good monaural, because it weighs less than 6 lbs. with batteries.

And as easy to operate because you don't have to swing out or detach any speakers.

The 9300WA has three speakers, but they're mounted side-by-side inside the radio.

They disperse the sound into the air in front of the radio, eliminating the "hole-in-the-middle" effect, and give you a much fuller sound than is possible from conventional, two-speaker stereo radios.

Why it doesn't need separated speakers to create stereo sound.

Besides three stereo speakers, the all-solid-state 9300WA has FM with AFC to driftproof your station, AM, stereo indicator light, and an AC cord.

Remember, though, it's not the three speakers that make it a great portable stereo radio.

It's the sound.

SONY

The SONY one-piece Portable Stereo Radio

Popular Music

Singer/songwriter **Don McLean's** enigmatic single *American Pie* tops many of the pop charts worldwide and stays at the #1 spot for 4 weeks in the U.S. The song's recurring lyric, "the day the music died" refers to the 1959 plane crash that killed Buddy Holly, The Big Bopper, and Ritchie Valens.

Roberta Flack

interprets a 1957 folk song, *The First Time Ever I Saw Your Face*. Her elegant recording earns the Record of the Year and Song of the Year Grammy Awards, and is ranked as the #1 Hot 100 single for the year 1972.

Glam rocker **David Bowie** attains a new level of international stardom with the launch of his Ziggy Stardust concert tour to promote his new studio album, *The Rise and Fall of Ziggy Stardust and the Spiders from Mars*.

1972 POPULAR SONGS BY CHART POSITION

The First Time Ever I Saw Your Face .... Roberta Flack
Alone Again (Naturally) .... Gilbert O'Sullivan
American Pie .... Don McLean
Without You .... Nilsson
Candy Man .... Sammy Davis Jr.
I Gotcha .... Joe Tex
Lean On Me .... Bill Withers
Baby Don't Get Hooked on Me .. Mac Davis
Brand New Key .... Melanie
Daddy Don't You Walk So Fast . Wayne Newton
Let's Stay Together .... Al Green
Brandy (You're a Fine Girl) ...... Looking Glass
Oh Girl .... Chi-Lites
Nice To Be With You .... Gallery
My Ding-A-Ling .... Chuck Berry
If Loving You Is Wrong I Don't Want To Be Right .... Luther Ingram
Heart Of Gold .... Neil Young
Betcha By Golly, Wow .... Stylistics
I'll Take You There .... Staple Singers
Ben .... Michael Jackson
The Lion Sleeps Tonight .... Robert John
Outa-space .... Billy Preston
Slippin' Into Darkness .... War
Long Cool Woman .... Hollies
How Do You Do .... Mouth & MacNeal
Song Sung Blue .... Neil Diamond
A Horse With No Name .... America
Popcorn .... Hot Butter
Everybody Plays The Fool .... Main Ingredient
Precious And Few .... Climax
Last Night I Didn't Get To Sleep At All .... 5th Dimension
Nights In White Satin .... Moody Blues
Go All The Way .... Raspberries
Back Stabbers .... O'Jays
Sunshine .... Jonathan Edwards
Day After Day .... Badfinger
Rocket Man .... Elton John
Morning Has Broken .... Cat Stevens
The City Of New Orleans .... Arlo Guthrie
Garden Party .... Rick Nelson
I Can See Clearly Now .... Johnny Nash
Burning Love .... Elvis Presley

Sammy Davis Jr.

America

Al Green

The 15th Annual Grammy Awards recognize accomplishments from 1972

GRAMMY awards

song of the year
The First Time Ever I Saw Your Face
Roberta Flack & Ewan MacColl (songwriter)

record of the year
The First Time Ever I Saw Your Face
Roberta Flack & Joel Dorn (producer)

album of the year
The Concert for Bangladesh
George Harrison (producer/artist), Phil Spector (producer),
Eric Clapton, Bob Dylan, Billy Preston & others

new artist
America

male pop vocal performance
Without You Harry Nilsson

female pop vocal performance
I Am Woman Helen Reddy

rhythm & blues song
Papa Was a Rollin' Stone The Temptations,
Barrett Strong & Norman Whitfield (songwriters)

country + western song
"Kiss an Angel Good Mornin'
Charley Pride, Ben Peters (songwriter)

Helen Reddy

The Temptations

new bands

ABBA

Alabama

Average White Band

Manhattan Transfer

Styx

Twisted Sister

Harvest
Neil Young

JACKSON BROWNE
LOS ANGELES, CALIFORNIA

The Original Motion Picture Soundtrack Written & Performed by
CURTIS MAYFIELD
THE SIG SHORE PRODUCTION
Super Fly
DIRECTOR GORDON PARKS, JR.
STARRING
RON O'NEAL
CARL LEE
JULIUS HARRIS
SHEILA FRAZIER
CHARLES McGREGOR
SIG SHORE PRODUCER
PHILLIP FENTY SCREENPLAY

1972

HENDRIX
IN THE
WEST

THE WORLD IS A GHETTO
WAR
JOE BURGERS

LOU REED-TRANSFORMER

MOTHERS
JUST ANOTHER BAND FROM L.A.

Bill Withers
SXBS 7014 STEREO
Still Bill

ROBERTA FLACK & DONNY HATHAWAY

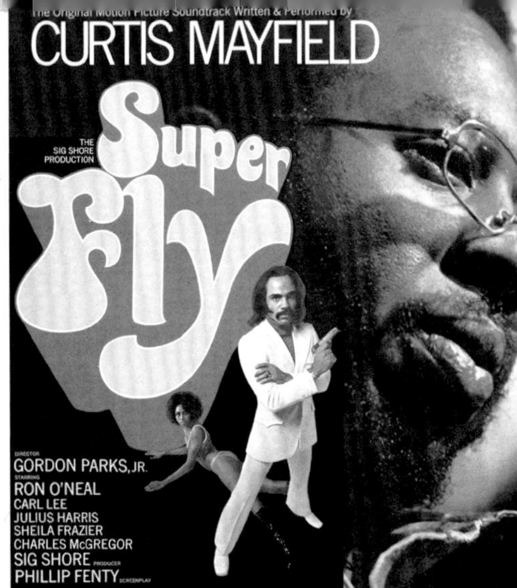

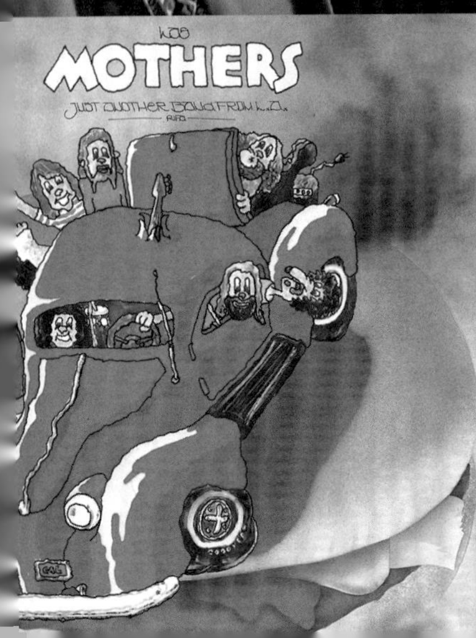

RECORD COLLECTION

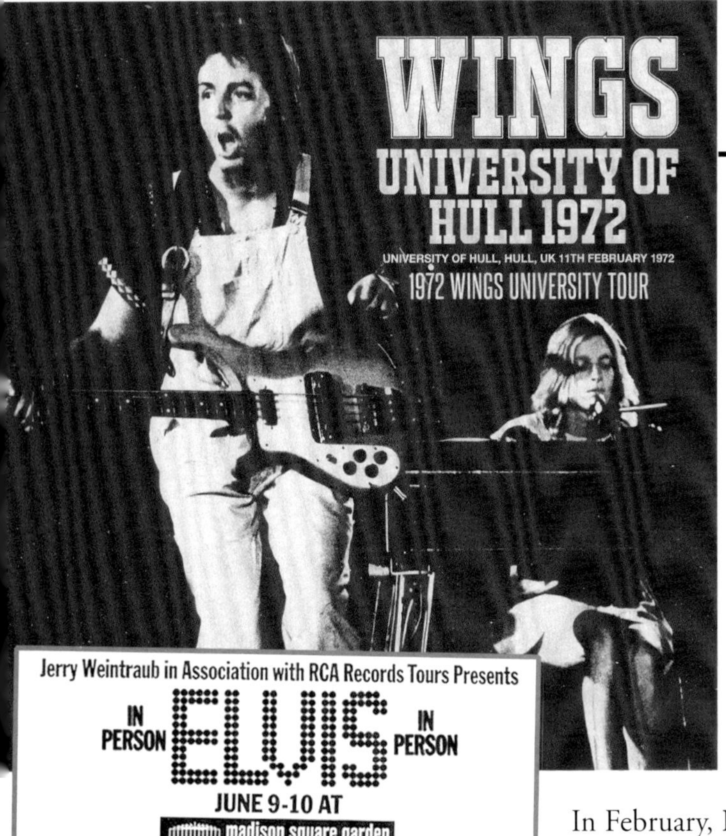

KEITH RICHARDS hops on stage to jam with **CHUCK BERRY** during a Hollywood Palladium concert, but is removed for playing too loud. Berry later expresses regret, saying that he didn't recognize the Rolling Stones guitarist.

In February, **PAUL MCCARTNEY** makes his post-Beatles live concert debut with his new band, Wings.

ELVIS PRESLEY'S four Madison Square Garden concerts sell out in one day.

SIMON & GARFUNKEL reunite for a live performance at Madison Square Garden to benefit the presidential campaign of George McGovern.

Several artists deliver LPs which will become recognized as hallmarks of their careers. **Neil Young's** *Harvest* marks his biggest success as a solo artist and includes classic tracks like "Old Man" and the #1 hit, "Heart of Gold."

Neil Young

The LP *Still Bill* by **Bill Withers** is a critical and commercial success and features some of the singer/songwriter's most popular songs, inclu-ding the hit singles "Lean on Me" and "Use Me."

Bill Withers

THE BLUES *Passings*

Davis

Rushing

Blues singer, guitarist and harmonica player **Reverend Gary Davis** (76) gained appreciation during the 1960s folk revival and influenced the likes of Bob Dylan and Dave Van Ronk.

Blues shouter and pianist **Jimmy Rushing** (70), affectionately known as "Mr. Five By Five," was a renowned vocalist with the Count Basie Orchestra.

DIED IN 1972

Over 40,000 mourners file past the open casket of gospel singer **Mahalia Jackson** (61) who passes away on January 27, 1972.

"Sidewinder" hard bop trumpeter **Lee Morgan** (33) is shot to death by his common-law wife outside a jazz club on February 19, 1972.

Drifters R&B singer, **Clyde McPhatter** (39) passes away from heart, liver & kidney disease, June 13, 1972.

Allman Brothers bassist **Berry Oakley** (24) is killed in a motorcycle accident, November 11, 1972, 3 blocks from the spot where Duane Allman died on a motorcycle in 1971.

BORN IN 1972 ★ ROB THOMAS ★ BILLIE JOE ARMSTRONG ★ TIMBALAND ★ COMMON ★ BUSTA RHYMES ★ NOTORIOUS B.I.G. ★ GERI HALLIWELL ★ LIAM GALLAGHER ★ EMINEM ★ BRAD PAISLEY ★ JOEY MCINTYRE

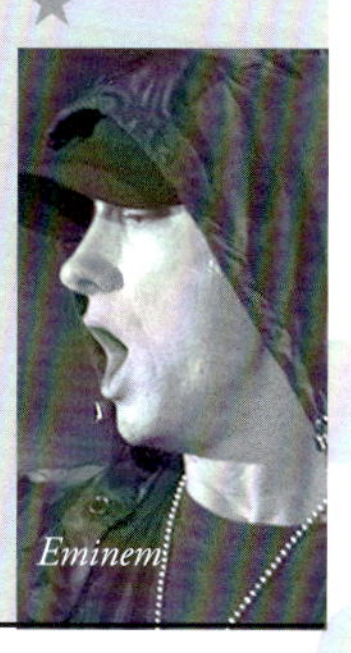

Eminem

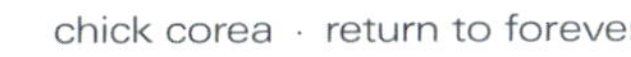

Chick Corea

Electric jazz and jazz fusion continue to be the dominant trends in 1972 improvisation-based recorded music. Now considered a fusion classic, pianist **Chick Corea's** *Return to Forever* LP is funky and soaring, and features vocalist Flora Purim & bassist Stanley Clarke. Trumpeter **Miles Davis** continues the funky jam with *On the Corner*, recognizing the influence of soulsters James Brown and Sly Stone. The influential group **Weather Report** cooks up *I Sing the Body Electric*. And, in a more classic jazz mode, pianist **McCoy Tyner** releases *Echoes of a Friend*, a gorgeous and dynamic live solo piano tribute to saxophone master John Coltrane, with whom Tyner spent his formative musical years.

Miles Davis

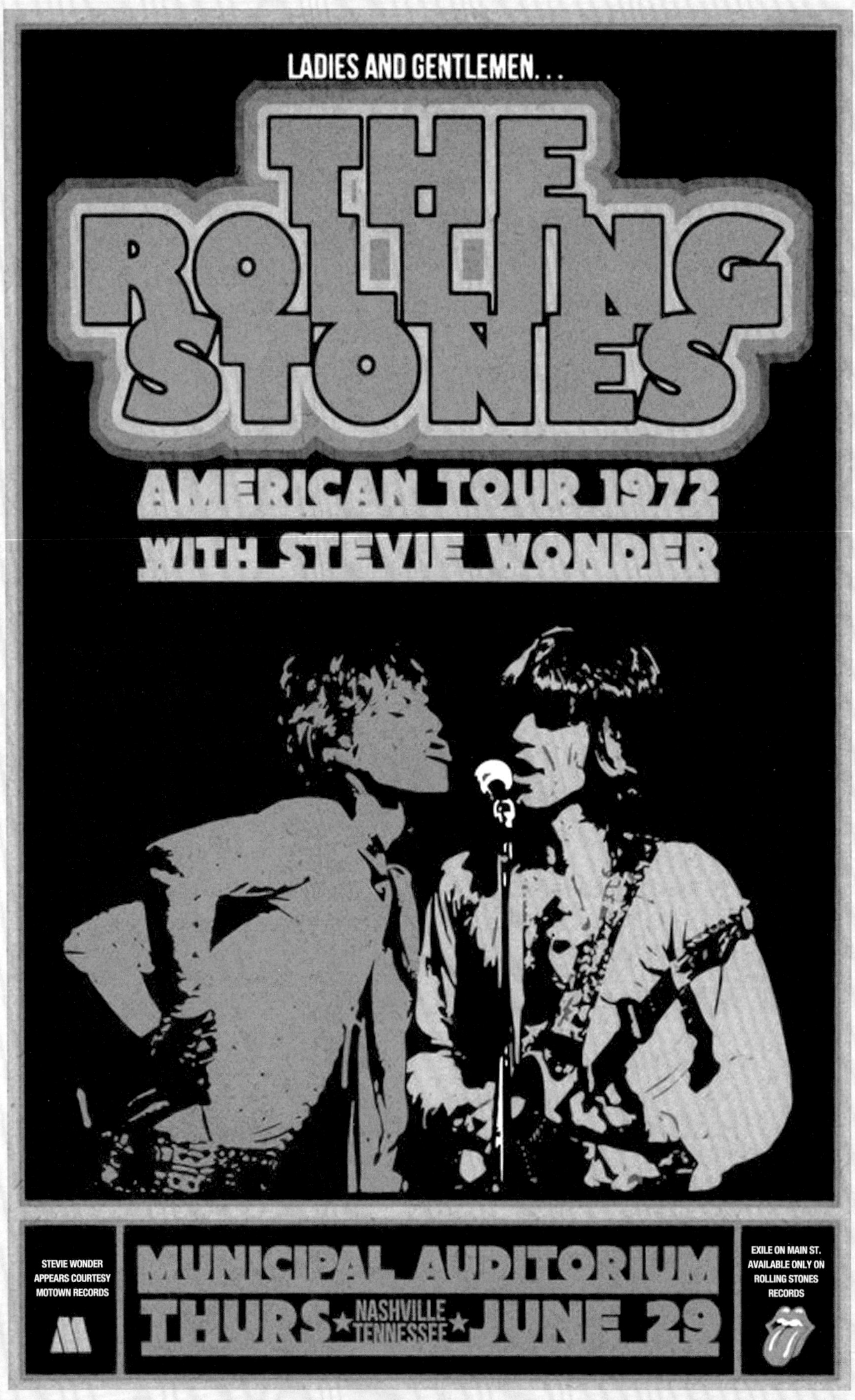
LADIES AND GENTLEMEN...
THE ROLLING STONES
AMERICAN TOUR 1972
WITH STEVIE WONDER
STEVIE WONDER
APPEARS COURTESY
MOTOWN RECORDS
EXILE ON MAIN ST.
AVAILABLE ONLY ON
ROLLING STONES
RECORDS
MUNICIPAL AUDITORIUM
THURS NASHVILLE TENNESSEE JUNE 29

COUNTRY & WESTERN #1 HITS

Carolyn / Grandma Harp	Merle Haggard
One's on the Way	Loretta Lynn
My Man (Understands)	Tammy Wynette
That's Why I Love You Like I Do ...	Sonny James
Chantilly Lace	Jerry Lee Lewis
Funny Face	Donna Fargo
My Hang-Up is You	Freddie Hart
Eleven Roses	Hank Williams Jr.
She's Got to Be a Saint	Ray Price
I Can't Stop Loving You	Conway Twitty
If You Leave Me Tonight I'll Cry ...	Jerry Wallace
I's Four in the Morning	Faron Young

Merle Haggard

is pardoned by California Governor Ronald Reagan for a 1957 robbery which had landed him in prison for two-and-a-half years, ending in 1960. In his younger years, Haggard was plagued by stints in detention centers for a lengthy series of crimes.

Left to right: Loretta Lynn, Sonny James, Tammy Wynette, Charley Pride

Country Music Awards

ENTERTAINER OF THE YEAR: Loretta Lynn / **TOP MALE VOCALIST:** Charley Pride / **TOP FEMALE VOCALIST:** Loretta Lynn / **TOP VOCAL DUO:** Conway Twitty & Loretta Lynn / **SINGLE OF THE YEAR:** *The Happiest Girl In the Whole USA* – Donna Fargo / **SONG OF THE YEAR:** *Easy Loving* – Freddie Hart / **INSTRUMENTALIST OF THE YEAR:** Charlie McCoy

OPRYLAND USA opens in Nashville, Tennessee. Billed as the "Home of American Music," it features a variety of music shows and amusement park rides such as roller coasters. It's creation was driven by a desire for a new, permanent, larger and more modern home for the long-running Grand Ole Opry radio program.

Ringo Starr's immaculate '57 Chevy hardtop customized by George Barris is up for grabs.

HOW YOU CAN WIN.

Just walk into any participating Craig dealer and sign up. If you don't win the car, there are over 1,000 other prizes you may win.

But hurry, the sweepstakes closes May 10.

WHAT'S ON THE INSIDE.

It's everything you'd expect. It features Craig's newest In-Dash Cassette AM/FM/MPX Radio with a digital readout that doubles as a clock when the radio is off. Plus Craig's new 72 Watt Powerplay" amp, with less than 0.5% THD and graphic equalizer, and the revolutionary Trans-Rib" speakers.

Naturally your Craig dealer will be happy to show you the system without the car.

All you have to do is walk into the store. And who knows, you may be riding home. CRAIG ®

34

Classical Music

German composer
Karlheinz Stockhausen
premieres two new compositions including **Alphabet für Liège**, which highlights sound vibrations and requires 4 hours to perform.

American composer
George Crumb

completes *Makrokosmos, Volume I , the first of 4 pieces for amplified piano influenced by composer Béla Bartók as well as the 12 signs of the Zodiac.*

Steve Reich's minimalist composition, *CLAPPING MUSIC,* is written for two performers and is performed entirely by clapping.

New Works

Metamorphic Variations
Arthur Bliss

Spiegel
Friedrich Cerha

A Letter to the 30th Century (oratorio)
Dimitri Kabalevsky

Bewegung
Peter Ruzicka

Distance
Toru Takemitsu

Curse Upon Iron
Veljo Tormis

Transientes for Orchestra
Mario Davidovsky

Symphony No. 4
Paul Le Flem

Recordanza for cello & piano
George Rochberg

Pulitzer Prize

Windows
Jacob Druckman

Murray David Perahia
is the first American pianist to win the
Leeds International Piano Competition

Opera News

An opera in one act, *The Trial of Mary Lincoln*, premieres on a nationally televised broadcast on February 14, 1972. A work of historical fiction, the opera is based on the 1875 trial in which the sanity of Mary Todd Lincoln was scrutinized. Composed by **Thomas Pasatieri** with a libretto by **Anne Howard Bailey**, it earns an Emmy Award for Outstanding Writing for a Variety Series. **Elaine Bonazzi** has the title role.

Elaine Bonazzi in The Trial of Mary Lincoln

PASSING

Michael Rabin
(May 2, 1936 –
January 19, 1972)
dies from a fall in his New York City apartment at 35. The American violinist, called one of the most talented of his generation, first played the Royal Albert Hall at the age of 18.

Anne Frank in a 1941 school photo

The Diary of Anne Frank, a monodrama (single actor) in 21 scenes for soprano and chamber orchestra, has its premiere. The production is based on the writings of the young Dutch diarist killed by the Nazis. Music and libretto are by **Grigory Frid**.

***T*reemonisha** is a 1911 opera by American ragtime composer, **Scott Joplin**. The work was largely unknown until it is given it's first complete performance by the Atlanta Symphony under **Robert Shaw**. Though sometimes called a "ragtime opera," *Treemonisha* incorporates multiple musical styles and includes choruses, small group pieces, a ballet and arias.

Louise Parker as Monisha in the Filene Center production of Treemonisha *and the 1911 Scott Joplin manuscript cover.*

PINK FLOYD
TOUR '72

ON BROADWAY

~ Greasers Hit the Stage ~

The Jim Jacobs / Warren Casey musical based on the 1950s high school Greaser subculture is a huge hit in its Broadway debut. Opening first in downtown Manhattan's Eden Theatre before moving to the Broadhurst, the original cast includes Barry Bostwick as Danny, Carole Demas as Sandy, and Adrienne Barbeau as Rizzo.

Cast of *Grease*

ANOTHER OPENING, ANOTHER NIGHT

Cast of *Don't Bother Me, I Can't Cope*

THE COUNTRY GIRL

LOST IN THE STARS

ALL THE GIRLS CAME OUT TO PLAY

AN EVENING WITH RICHARD NIXON AND...

JACQUES BREL IS ALIVE AND WELL AND LIVING IN PARIS

THE LAST OF MRS. LINCOLN

CHILDREN! CHILDREN!

PURLIE

Pippin Pops!

Ben Vereen leads the cast of Pippin as Leading Player, who conveys the story of the young prince Pippin (John Rubinstein) as he searches for the meaning of life. Bob Fosse directs and choreographs. The musical hit runs for 1,944 performances, snagging 5 Tonys and 5 Drama Desk awards.

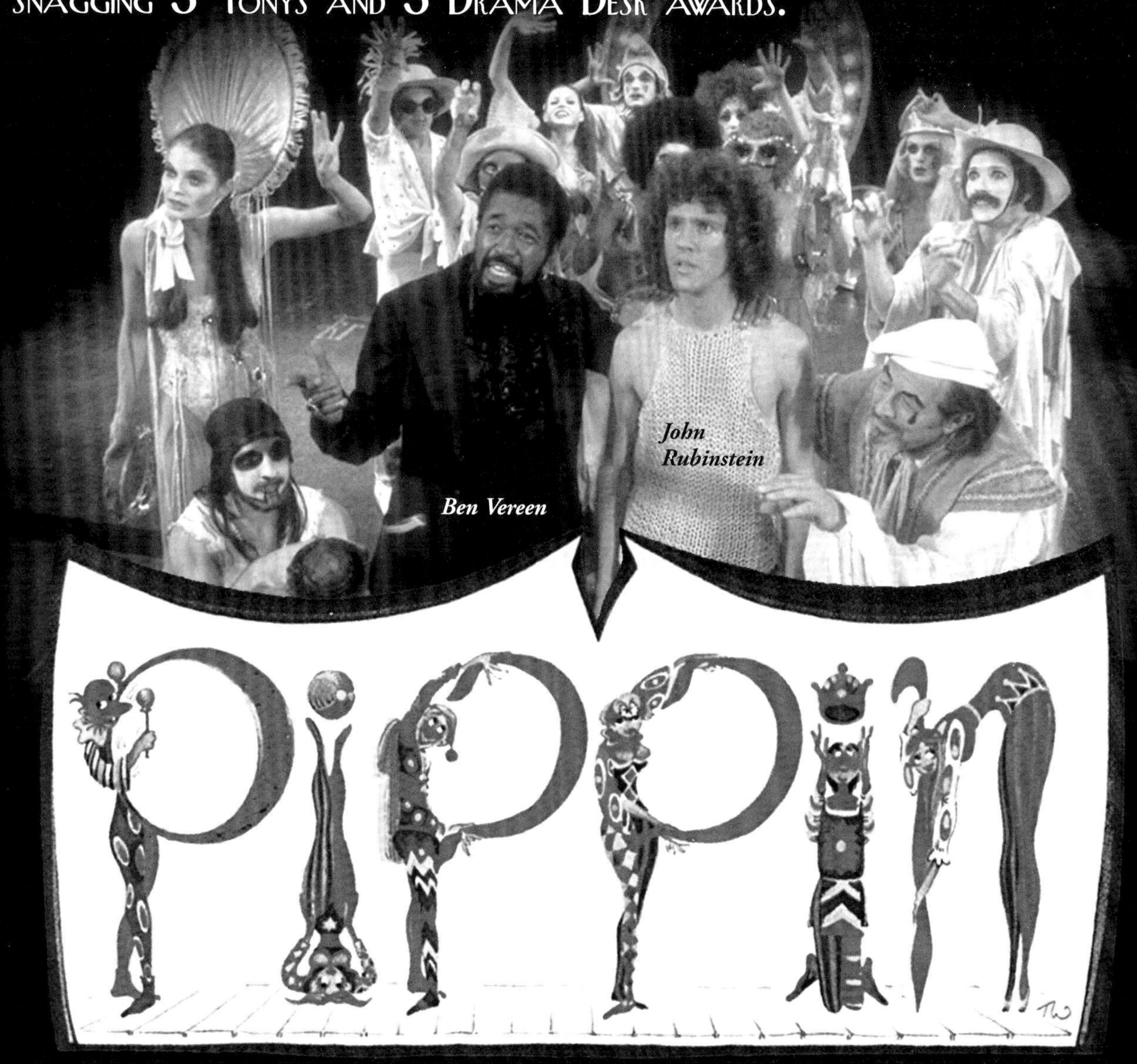

flops galore

These 1972 musicals seemed like good ideas at the time, but they fall flat. Both feature music by **Hair** *composer Galt MacDermot.*

Dude

Oct 9 - Oct 21, 1972. The *New York Times* says *Dude* "may go down in theatrical history as Broadway's most monumental disaster."

Via Galactica

Nov 28 - Dec 02, 1972. This short-lived science fiction spectacle with an incomprehensible plot closes after seven performances.

Tony Awards

27th Annual Tony Awards held on March 25, 1973 for 1972 productions

BEST PLAY
"That Championship Season"
Jason Miller (playwright)

BEST MUSICAL
"A Little Night Music"
H. Wheeler (book) S. Sondheim (music)

BEST ACTOR in a PLAY
Alan Bates
"Butley"

BEST ACTRESS in a PLAY
Julie Harris
"The Last of Mrs. Lincoln"

BEST DIRECTOR - PLAY
A.J. Antoon
"That Championship Season"

BEST ACTOR in a MUSICAL
Ben Vereen
"Pippin"

BEST ACTRESS in a MUSICAL
Glynnis Johns
"A Little Night Music"

BEST DIRECTOR - MUSICAL
Bob Fosse
"Pippin"

BEST CHOREOGRAPHY
Bob Fosse
"Pippin"

NO PULITZER PRIZE For DRAMA is AWARDED in 1972

WHAT ELSE IS PLAYING:

Fun City

✵

There's One in Every Marriage

✵

Wise Child

✵

The Love Suicide

✵

Moonchildren

✵

Night Watch

✵

Sticks and Bones

✵

Twelfth Night

✵

The Selling of the President

✵

Voices

✵

A Funny Thing Happened on the Way to the Forum

✵

That's Entertainment

WHAT ELSE IS PLAYING:

Elizabeth I

✵

Sugar

✵

The Little Black Book

✵

Ring Around the Bathtub

✵

Different Times

✵

Tough to Get Help

✵

Heathen!

✵

From Israel with Love

✵

Hurry, Harry

✵

The Lincoln Mask

✵

Dear Oscar

✵

Butley

✵

The Sunshine Boys

✵

Don Juan

Film makers Dennis Hopper and John Huston. Different generations but each a master of his craft.

In 1941, a young maverick of a man directed his first motion picture.
The man was John Huston. The motion picture was "The Maltese Falcon," a masterpiece that's had profound and lasting influence on the making of films.
In 1969, another young maverick of a man directed a motion picture, also his first.
This time it was Dennis Hopper and "Easy Rider." Both the man and his film have made an extraordinary impact on the minds, imaginations and life styles of people everywhere.
Huston. And Hopper.
Different generations. But with a common desire. Each wants to be the best there is, a leader in his craft.
The beams are that way, too. And for 177 years now, they've *been* the best there is, leaders in their craft—the distilling of Kentucky Bourbon.
A proud record.
A proud Bourbon. Smooth and light and mellow, with a rich aroma full of promise.
Jim Beam. For six generations; one family, one formula, one purpose. The world's finest Bourbon.

Generation gap? JIM BEAM never heard of it.

BEAM
SINCE 1795
THE WORLD'S FINEST BOURBON
JIM BEAM
Sour Mash
KENTUCKY · STRAIGHT
BOURBON WHISKEY
Distilled and bottled by
JAMES B BEAM DISTILLING CO.
CLERMONT BEAM
KENTUCKY
SINCE 1795

The world's finest Bourbon since 1795.

86 PROOF KENTUCKY STRAIGHT BOURBON WHISKEY DISTILLED AND BOTTLED BY THE JAMES B. BEAM DISTILLING CO., CLERMONT, BEAM, KENTUCKY

At The MUSEUM

Vandal!

Bystanders subdue the attacker

May 21, 1972 — In the Vatican's St. Peter's Basilica, Hungarian-born Australian Laszlo Toth (33) attacks **Michelangelo's *Pietà*** statue with a hammer, shouting that he is Jesus Christ. He is subdued by bystanders but not before raining 15 blows on the marble, removing Mary's arm and chipping her face. Toth is committed to a psychiatric hospital.

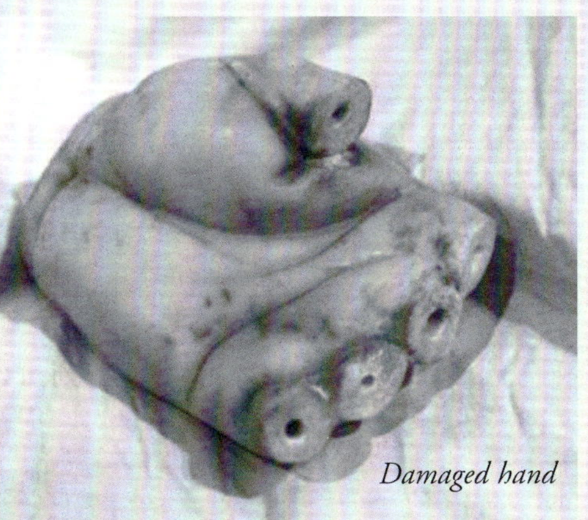

Damaged hand

Art Thieves!

Sept 4, 1972 — Three armed robbers use a skylight under repair to gain entry to the Montreal Museum of Fine Arts, tie up three guards, and make off with 18 paintings, including a rare **Rembrandt** landscape and pieces by **Jan Brueghel the Elder, Corot, Delacroix, Rubens** and **Thomas Gainsborough**. None of the works, valued at millions, have ever been recovered and no arrests made. Some speculate that the "Skylight Caper" is an inside job.

Rembrandt's Landscape with Cottages

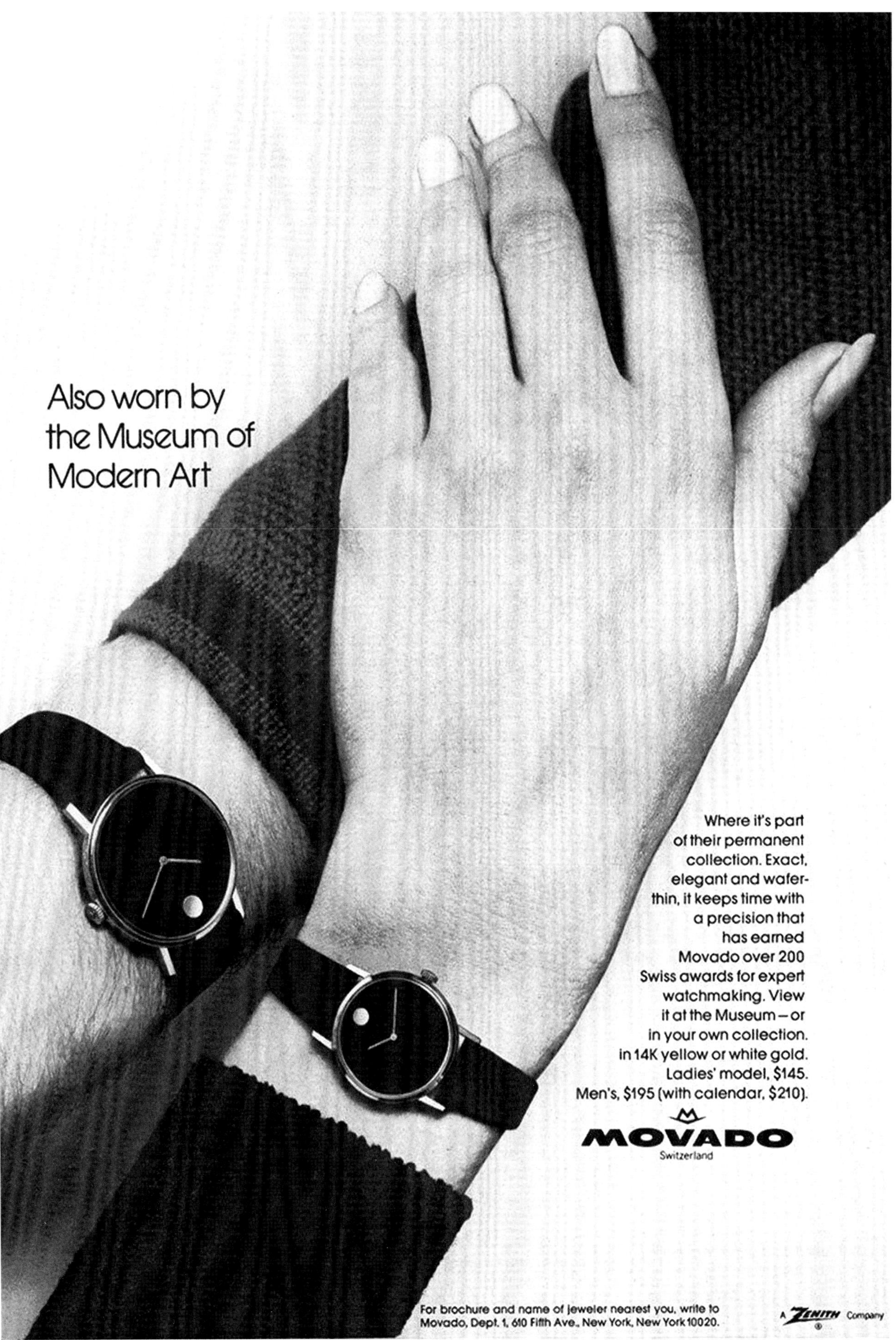
Also worn by
the Museum of
Modern Art
Where it's part
of their permanent
collection. Exact,
elegant and wafer-
thin, it keeps time with
a precision that
has earned
Movado over 200
Swiss awards for expert
watchmaking. View
it at the Museum — or
in your own collection.
In 14K yellow or white gold.
Ladies' model, $145.
Men's, $195 (with calendar, $210).
MOVADO
Switzerland
For brochure and name of jeweler nearest you, write to
Movado, Dept. 1, 610 Fifth Ave., New York, New York 10020.
A ZENITH Company

Joplin at the Turn of the Century, 1896-1906 is a 1972 mural by renowned American Regionalist painter **Thomas Hart Benton**, depicting people on the Main Street of Joplin, Missouri at the turn of the century. The 14-foot-wide painting is installed at Joplin City Hall.

1972 Art Highlights

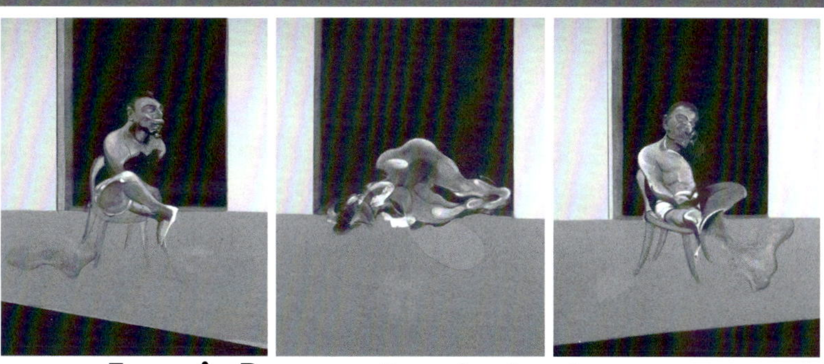

Francis Bacon – *Triptych*, oil on 3 canvases

David Hockney – *Pool with 2 Figures*, acrylic on canvas

Christo – *Valley Curtain*, orange curtain along Colorado State Hwy 325

NEW INSTITUTIONS

Designed by Louis Kahn, the Kimbell Art Museum in Fort Worth, TX, is opened.

Kimbell Museum

The Kunsten Museum of Modern Art Aalborg, Denmark, designed by Alvar and Elissa Aalto and Jean-Jacques Baruël, is completed.

A.I.R. Gallery at 97 Wooster Street, SoHo, New York, is the first artist-run, not-for-profit gallery for women artists in the United States.

Twenty pochoir stencil plates from French artist **Henri Matisse's** 1947 portfolio *Jazz* are the subject of a 1972 exhibit at New York's Museum of Modern Art.

PASSINGS

M.C. Escher, Hand with Reflecting Sphere, 1935

Dutch printmaker/graphic artist **Maurice Cornelis (M.C.) Escher** dies at the age of 73. While underappreciated in his early years, he later gained renown for his mathematically inspired woodcuts, lithographs, and mezzotints depicting "impossible objects" and expressions of infinity and intriguing geometry.

Surrealist Assemblage artist **Joseph Cornell** passes away, aged 69. His "boxes" are influential and widely admired, though Cornell was a recluse who rarely ventured beyond his New York basement.

Joseph Cornell, A Parrot for Juan Gris, 1953

Books

Ezra Pound, 87, American poet and critic.

Heinrich Böll

Hunter S. Thompson's famous work of "gonzo journalism," *Fear and Loathing in Las Vegas: A Savage Journey to the Heart of the American Dream*, is issued as a book after being serialized in *Rolling Stone* magazine. **Ralph Steadman's** illustrations vividly capture the drug-addled road trip of Raoul Duke, and his attorney, Dr. Gonzo.

British veterinary surgeon **James Herriot's** (James Alfred Wight) animal stories are combined into a single volume titled *All Creatures Great and Small*, leading to huge sales and a franchise including film and TV series.

NOBEL PRIZE FOR LITERATURE
Heinrich Böll

PULITZER PRIZE
FICTION
ANGLE OF REPOSE
Wallace Stegner
POETRY
COLLECTED POEMS
James Wright

BOOKER PRIZE
G.
John Berger

CARLOS CASTANEDA
JOURNEY TO IXTLAN
The Lessons of Don Juan
By the author of A Separate Reality

Watership
Down
A novel by
Richard Adams

CHARLIE AND
THE GREAT GLASS
ELEVATOR
ROALD DAHL

MARTIN AMIS
the
RACHEL
PAPERS
'EXTRAVAGANTLY
SEXUAL . . .
HIGHLY
ENJOYABLE'
EVENING STANDARD
Panther
586 04120 6

THE
TERMINAL
MAN
A NOVEL BY
MICHAEL CRICHTON

The
Manticore
A Novel
ROBERTSON DAVIES
Author of FIFTH BUSINESS

FREDERICK
FORSYTH
AUTHOR OF THE DAY OF THE JACKAL
THE
ODESSA
FILE

Graham
Greene
Graham Greene
The Honorary Consul
The
Honorary
Consul
A Novel

The Stepford
Wives
New Novel by the Author of Rosemary's Baby
Ira Levin

Ludlum
The Osterman Weekend
The
Osterman
Weekend
A Novel by
Robert
Ludlum
author of The Scarlatti Inheritance

VLADIMIR
NABOKOV
TRANSPARENT
THINGS
A New Novel
by the
Author of LOLITA
and ADA

My Name is Asher Lev
My
Name
is
Asher
Lev
Chaim Potok
Chaim Potok

THE GODS THEM-
SELVES
a novel by
ISAAC ASIMOV

The Friends of
Eddie Coyle
A Novel by
George V. Higgins

P.D.JAMES An
Unsuitable
Job for a
Woman

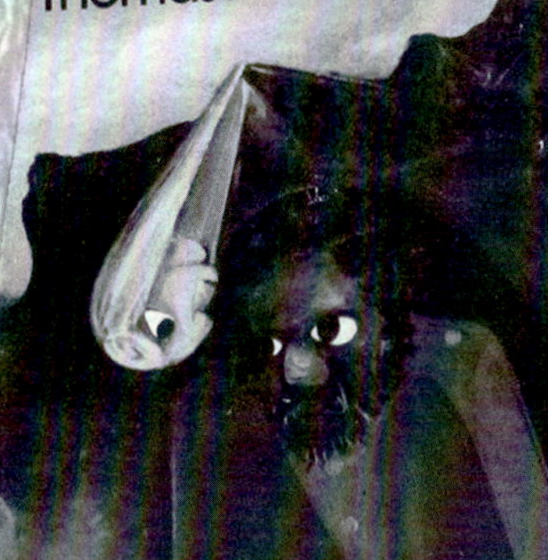

Irving Wallace
THE
WORD

TAYLOR
CALDWEL
CAPTAINS
AND
THE
KINGS
A NOVEL ABOUT
AN AMERICAN

architecture

AIA Gold Medal

American Institute of Architects

- 1972 -
Pietro Belluschi

AIA Twenty-Five Year Award

Conferred on **Baldwin Hills Village** in Los Angeles. Designed in the late '30s, it is one of the oldest planned communities of its type in the nation.

Baldwin administration building

The South Tower of New York's World Trade Center opens to tenants. At 1,362 feet, it is the world's second tallest building. **Minoru Yamasaki** is the architect. The North Tower is also completed in 1972.

The **TRANSAMERICA PYRAMID** is completed in **San Francisco**.

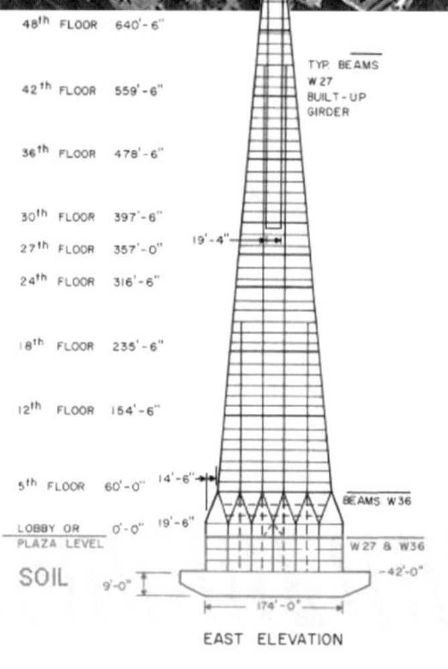

The **OLYMPIASTADION** for the 1972 Summer Olympics is completed in **Munich**.

and design

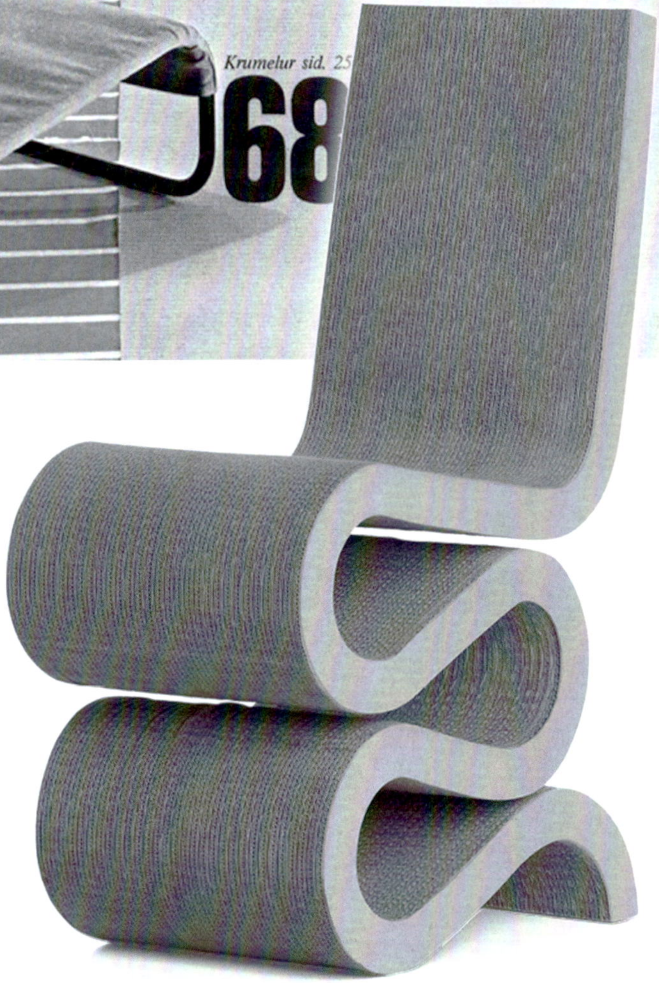

Frank Gehry laminated
cardboad "Wiggle Chair"

The less you spend on a car, the more you can spend on other things.

This car gets up to 40 miles to the gallon.

Up to 75 miles an hour.

Overhead cam engine, rack and pinion steering, 4-speed synchromesh transmission, power-assisted front disc brakes, front bucket seats, radial tires, tachometer, racing mirror. All standard equipment.

Oh, it doesn't have automatic transmission, air conditioning, and a 400-horsepower engine.

But which would you rather have? Automatic transmission, air conditioning, and a 400-horsepower engine?

Or Michelle and Tammy and Alison?

The Honda Coupe. Under $1700.*
It makes a lot of sense.

*SUGGESTED RETAIL P.O.E. DEALER PREPARATION, TRANSPORTATION, TAX AND LICENSE EXTRA. ©1972 AMERICAN HONDA MOTOR CO., INC.

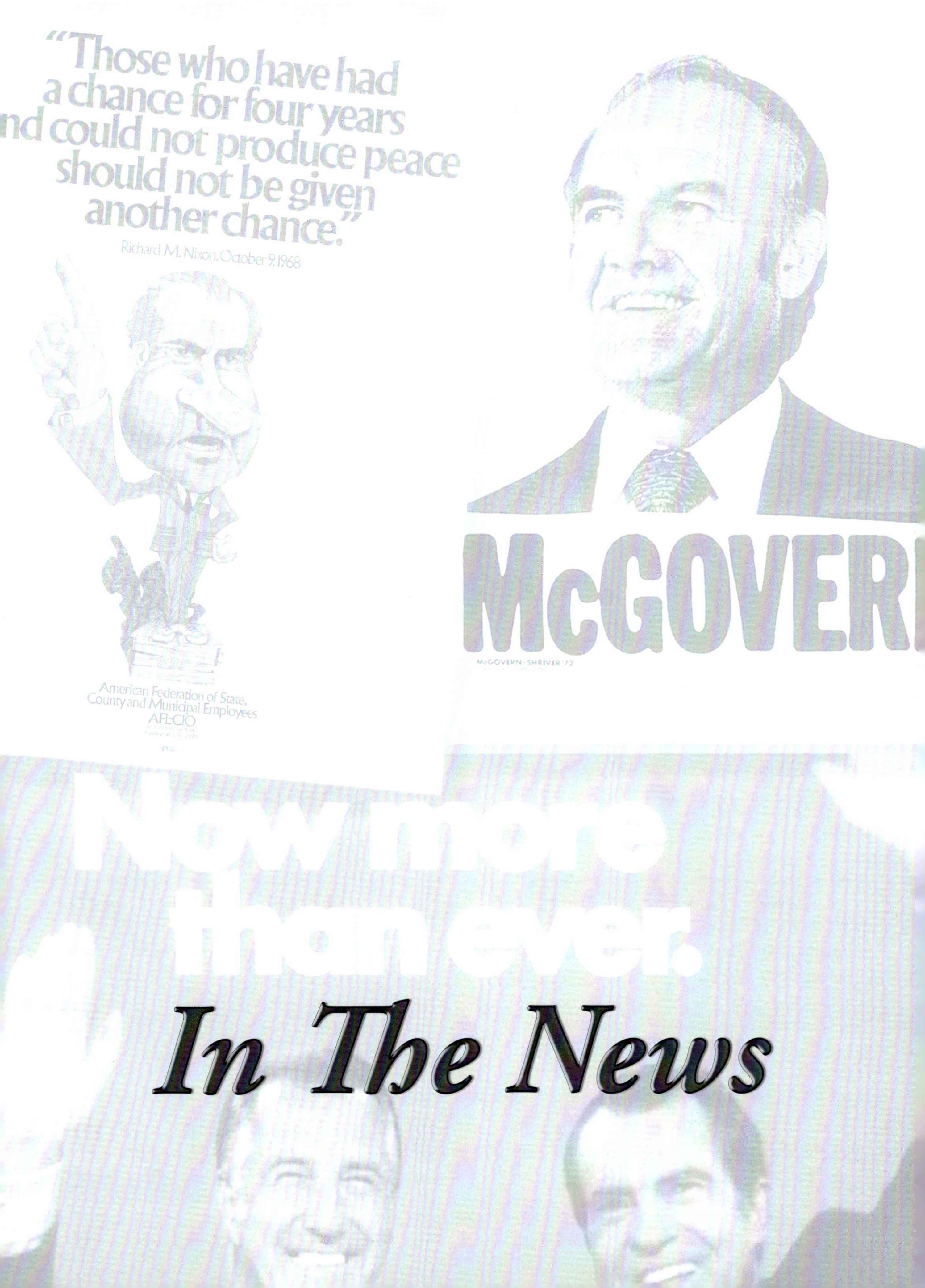
"Those who have had
a chance for four years
nd could not produce peace
should not be given
another chance."
Richard M. Nixon, October 9, 1968
American Federation of State,
County and Municipal Employees
AFL-CIO
McGOVER
McGOVERN-SHRIVER '72
Now more
than ever.

In The News

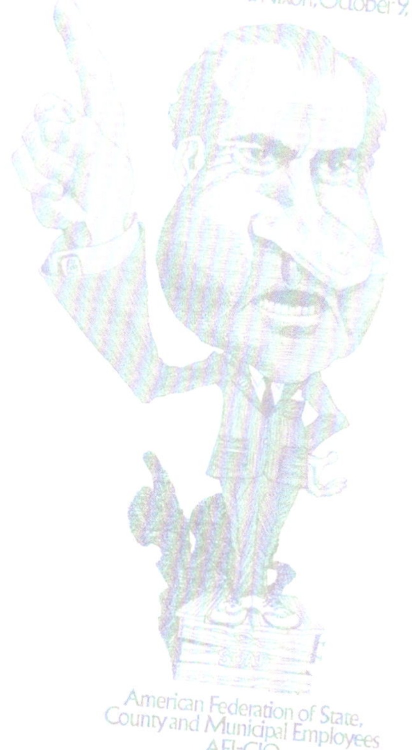

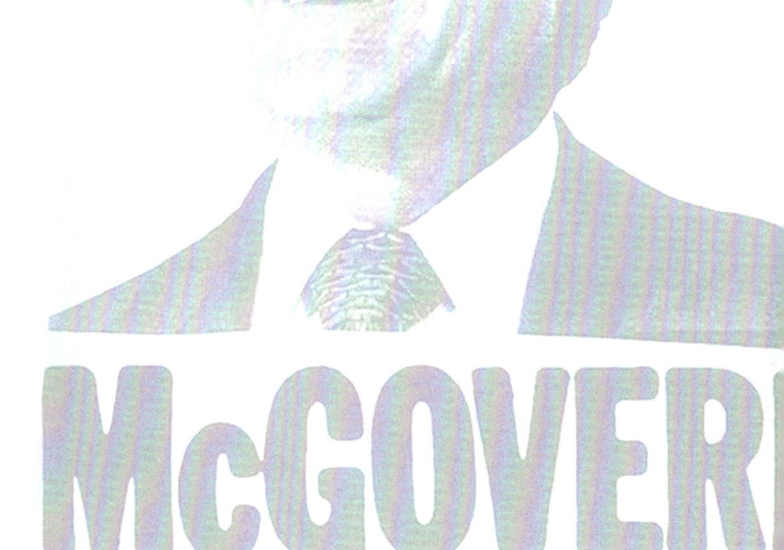

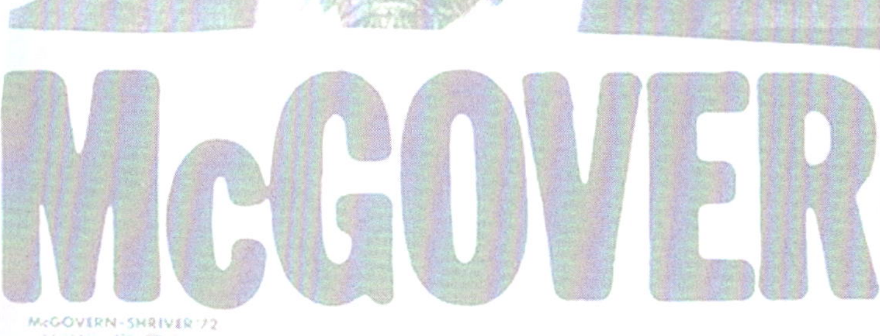

Nixon in China

In February, U.S. President Richard Nixon embarks on an 8-day visit to the People's Republic of China, becoming the first American President to do so. He visits three cities, including Beijing, and meets with Chairman Mao Zedong and Premier Zhou Enlai. The visit is regarded as a diplomatic breakthrough.

Nixon & Mao

Opening the People's Republic of China is a top priority of the Nixon administration. An unexpected opportunity presented itself with the 1971 World Table Tennis Championships in Nagoya, Japan. Good will between the U.S. and Chinese teams prompted Chairman **Mao Zedong** to invite the U.S. team on an all-expense paid visit to China. 15 American table tennis players and their entourage crossed the "Bamboo Curtain," leading President Nixon to announce an easing of U.S. travel bans and trade embargos against China and paving the way for Nixon's historic 1972 visit.

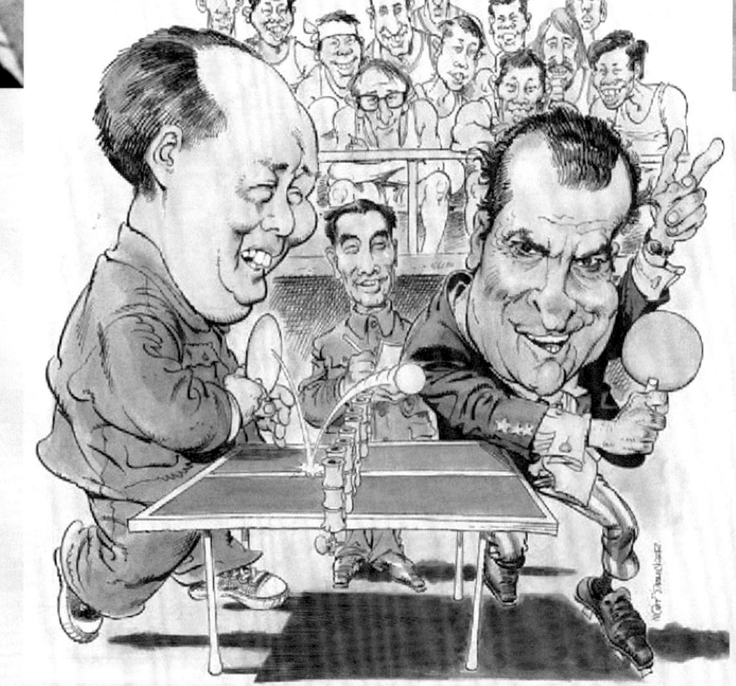

Mao Zedong and Richard Nixon from the National Portrait Gallery
© Mort Drucker.

POLITICS and WORLD EVENTS

The WATERGATE BREAK-IN

Watergate burglars, known as the "White House Plumbers": James McCord, Jr., Virgilio Gonzalez, Frank Sturgis, Eugenio Martinez, Bernard Barker & chief operative G. Gordon Liddy.

Five men are arrested in June for burglarizing the offices of the Democratic National Committee at the Washington D.C. Watergate Office Complex under the direction of the White House. President **Richard Nixon** and White House chief of staff **H. R. Haldeman** are later taped plotting to obstruct the FBI's investigation into the break-ins. In September, a grand jury indicts the five office burglars, as well as operatives **Howard Hunt** and **G. Gordon Liddy**. The Watergate Scandal leads to hearings and, eventually, the 1974 resignation of the President.

The WATERGATE **BREAK-IN**

The Gaslighting of Martha Mitchell

Martha Mitchell

Acontroversial and often misrepresented figure during the Watergate Scandal, **Martha Mitchell** — wife of U.S. Attorney General and head of the Committee to Re-Elect the President (CRP), **John Mitchell** — is alarmed when she learns of the Nixon campaign's involvement in the Watergate burglary.

Despite her husband's strong-arm efforts to keep her in the dark and isolated, Martha makes telephone contact with United Press reporter **Helen Thomas**. That phone call is cut off abruptly, with John Mitchell later telling reporter Thomas that "[Martha] gets a little upset about politics…"

Days later a reportedly severely bruised Martha says that she had been tranquilized and held captive in a hotel to keep her quiet. Though she is dismissed by Nixon aides as an unstable woman with a drinking problem, she continues to speak candidly with the press about the campaign's dirty tricks.

A photograph of the Watergate office complex entered into evidence at the burglary trial

The WATERGATE **BREAK-IN**

Woodward, Bernstein and Deep Throat

Bob Woodward

Carl Bernstein

Washington Post reporters **Bob Woodward** and **Carl Bernstein** are relatively unknown when they begin their investigative coverage of the Watergate break-in. They are aided in their work by a secret source nicknamed "Deep Throat," later revealed as FBI deputy director **Mark Felt**. In underground parking garage meetings, Deep Throat conveys the enormity of the coverup, including the involvement of former CIA officer **E. Howard Hunt**, the misappropriation of funds and the destruction of records. Woodward and Bernstein's buried scoops soon turn into increasingly consequential front-page headlines.

VIETNAMIZATION

With public opinion increasingly opposed to the Vietnam War, the **Richard Nixon** administration's Vietnamization policy, aimed at ending America's combat mission, achieves a limited rollback of Communist gains inside South Vietnam. The goal is primarily to provide the arms, training and funding for the South to fight and win its own war. Meanwhile, dead-locked peace talks in Paris between the U.S., North Vietnam, South Vietnam, and the Viet Cong enter their fifth year, finally beginning to make a bit of headway. In May, Nixon makes a major concession by accepting a cease-fire in exchange for a U.S. military withdrawal without requiring North Vietnam to do the same. By year-end, the number of U.S. military personnel in South Vietnam totals 24,200, down from more than 500,000 four years earlier.

March - October - The Easter Offensive: North Vietnam launches a major assault against South Vietnamese and U.S. troops in order to gain territory within the Demilitarized Zone (DMZ) and to obtain a better bargaining position at the Paris Peace Talks.

May - Operation Pocket Money: President Nixon orders the mining of Haiphong Harbor and the resumption of the bombing of Hanoi.

June - President Richard Nixon announces that no new draftees will be sent to Vietnam.

November - The U.S. Army turns over the massive Long Binh military base to South Vietnam.

December - The last draft lottery is held on December 7, 1972. These draft candidates are never called to duty and the authority to induct expires the following year.

The U.S. launches the Christmas bombing of North Vietnam from December 18th to the 29th against targeted complexes in the Hanoi and Haiphong areas. With peace close at hand, many nations denounce the bombings.

*A Pulitzer Prize is awarded to Associated Press photographer **Nick Ut** for the shocking scene he captured on June 8, 1972 showing a nine-year-old girl running naked after being severely burned on her back by a South Vietnamese napalm attack.*

Which man would you vote for?

Ah yes, what could be more dazzling than watching the candidates parade about, kissing babies and flashing winning smiles.

Consider the man in the top picture.

He promises to spend your tax dollars wisely.

But see how he spends his campaign dollars.

On a very fancy convertible.

Resplendent with genuine leather seats. A big 425-horsepower engine.

And a price tag that makes it one of the most expensive convertibles you can buy.

Now consider his opponent.

He promises to spend your tax dollars wisely.

But see how he spends his campaign dollars.

On a Volkswagen Convertible.

Resplendent with a hand-fitted top.

A warranty and four free diagnostic check-ups that cover you for 24 months or 24,000 miles.*

And a price tag that makes it one of the least expensive convertibles you can buy.

So maybe this year you'll find a politician who'll do what few politicians ever do:

Keep his promises before he's elected.

Anti-War Protests

Vietnam Veterans Against the War (VVAW) logo.

Antiwar protests in Auckland, New Zealand, left, and at the University of Michigan.

Antiwar demonstrations, both peaceful and violent, continue across the nation and around the world, with hundreds of thousands participating in major cities across the U.S. In April, Vietnam veterans throw over 700 medals on the steps of the U.S. Capitol building as 500,000 marchers join the protest.

Folksinger **Joan Baez** *(below)* joins **Coretta Scott King** at the Women Strike for Peace anti-war demonstration in Washington. At the end of 1972 Baez travels to Hanoi where she witnesses the Christmas bombing aerial attack.

Actress **Jane Fonda** *(right)* travels to Vietnam, where she is dubbed "Hanoi Jane" after being photographed at the seat of a North Vietnamese anti-aircraft gun. Later, she says she was manipulated into the photo and she apologizes. "It was never my intention to cause harm."

Election '72

Incumbent Republican President **Richard Nixon** from California defeats Democratic U.S. Senator **George McGovern** of South Dakota in the 1972 United States presidential election, held on Tuesday, November 7, 1972. Nixon campaigns on a strong economy and his success in foreign affairs, while McGovern calls for an immediate end to the Vietnam War. With only 55% of the electorate voting, Nixon wins in a landslide, taking over 60% of the popular vote and carrying 49 states, and is the first Republican to sweep the South. McGovern earns just 37.5% of the popular vote. 1972 marks the first presidential election in which the voting age is lowered from 21 to 18.

Within two years of the election, both Nixon and Vice President **Spiro Agnew** resign from office: Agnew in October 1973 for corruption involving criminal conspiracy, bribery, extortion and tax fraud, and Nixon in August 1974, over the evolving Watergate scandal.

Shirley Chisholm, the first black woman elected to the U.S. Congress, announces in January of 1972 that she will stand as a candidate for President.

Eagleton   Shriver

McGovern drops his Vice-Presidential running mate, **Thomas Eagleton**, when it is revealed that he underwent electroconvulsive therapy for depression. He is replaced by **Sargent Shriver**.

The Munich Massacre

A Palestinian terrorist group calling itself Black September invades the Olympic Village on September 5th during the 1972 Summer Olympics in Munich, Germany. They kill eleven Israeli athletes and one West German police officer after demanding the release of hundreds of jailed Palestinian and Red Faction prisoners, and safe passage to the airport. Five of the eight Palestinians are killed and three Palestinians are captured in a failed hostage rescue attempt.

On October 29th, Lufthansa Flight 615 is hijacked by Palestinian terrorists, who demand that the three surviving Munich perpetrators be turned over to them in exchange for the safety of the passengers. The West German government complies with the demands, a decision subject to much international criticism. Israel commences a years-long covert campaign, dubbed Operation Wrath of God, to track down and assasinate those responsible for the Munich Massacre.

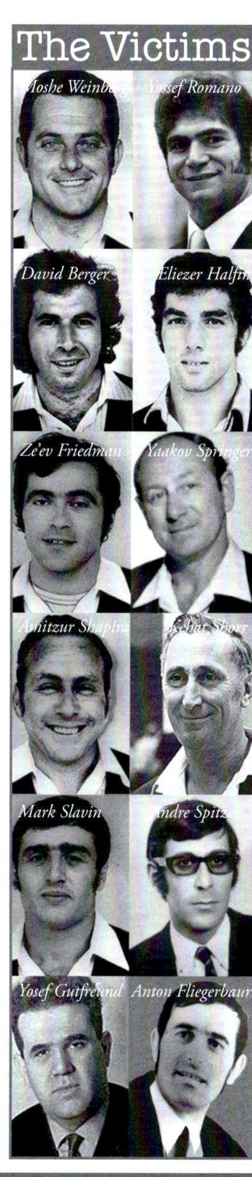

A Palestinian terrorist appears on a balcony.

The Lod Airport Massacre

Three members of the Japanese Red Army open fire with assault rifles and toss grenades at Israel's Lod Airport on May 30, 1972. The Japanese Red Army is a militant communist terrorist group recruited for the attack by a Palestinian organization called the Popular Front for the Liberation of Palestine. Twenty-six people are killed and 80 wounded. The dead are 17 U.S. citizens from Puerto Rico, 8 Israelis, and 1 Canadian citizen. Two of the attackers are killed and one is apprehended.

We'll pay you $42.76 to go to meetings.

There's more money today in the Army Reserve.

As a private with over four months service, you'll earn $42.76 a weekend. And your pay goes up as you go up.

In the Reserve things are happening faster these days. It's easier to get in—the waiting lists have vanished. It's easier to get promoted—the men who served in World War II are retiring.

It's always paid to go to meetings in the Army Reserve. Now it pays more.

The Army Reserve. It pays to go to meetings.

The United Nations launches the **Biological Weapons Convention (BWC)**, a disarmament treaty that bans the development, production, acquisition, transfer, stockpiling and use of biological and toxin weapons.

In June, The UN Conference on the Human Environment is held in Stockholm, Sweden, leading to the **United Nations Environment Programme (UNEP)**.

In November, the United Nations Educational, Scientific and Cultural Organization (UNESCO) adopts the **Convention Concerning the Protection of the World Cultural and Natural Heritage**.

The UN declares:

Human rights must be asserted, apartheid and colonialism condemned;

Natural resources must be safeguarded;

The Earth's capacity to produce renewable resources must be maintained;

Wildlife must be safeguarded;

Non-renewable resources must be shared and not exhausted;

Pollution must not exceed the environment's capacity to clean itself;

Damaging oceanic pollution must be prevented;

Developing countries need assistance;

Weapons of mass destruction must be eliminated.

UNITED NATIONS

NEW SECRETARY-GENERAL

Austrian **Kurt Waldheim** begins his first term as the fourth Secretary-General of the United Nations. Waldheim will serve two terms.

DICTATOR RANT

Ugandan dictator **Idi Amin** sends an anti-Semitic telegram to Secretary-General Waldheim, in which he applauds the massacre of the Israeli Olympic athletes in Munich and says Germany was the most appropriate locale for this because it was where Hitler burned more than six million Jews. He also calls to to expel Israel from the United Nations and to send all the Israelis to Britain, which bears the guilt for creating the Jewish state.

XXX THE TROUBLES XXX

Since the 1960s, Northern Ireland has been beset with strife arising from conflict between the Protestant Loyalists, who want Northern Ireland to remain within the United Kingdom, and the Catholic Irish Republicans, who want Northern Ireland to leave the United Kingdom and join a united Ireland. In 1972, explosions of political violence continue to rock the region. As the year opens, 29 barricades block access to "Free Derry," with the IRA (Irish Republican Army) patrolling the "no-go" areas. Hundreds of Irish Republican Nationalists are detained in prison without trial.

The British Army kills 14 unarmed nationalist civil rights marchers in Derry, Northern Ireland, on January 30th, a day dubbed "Bloody Sunday."

In February, Anti-British riots take place throughout Ireland. The British Embassy in Dublin is burned to the ground. An official IRA bomb kills seven in Aldershot, UK. The British government suspends the Parliament of Northern Ireland and introduces 'Direct Rule' of Northern Ireland in March. In July, 22 bombs planted by the Provisional IRA explode in Belfast, Northern Ireland, killing 9 and injuring over a hundred.

Left, Irish Republican Army poster; right, Ulster Volunteer Force mural; below left, mural depiction of Bloody Sunday; below right, mural of Bloody Sunday victims.

Norway rejects membership in the European Economic Community (EEC).

Margrethe II is the first Queen of Denmark since 1412. She succeeds her father, King Frederick IX, on the throne.

The "Cod War" breaks out between Britain and Iceland over fishing rights. Royal Navy ships protect British trawlers.

England's Queen Elizabeth II visits Yugoslavia, meeting President Tito.

The Federal Republic of Germany and German Democratic Republic (GDR) recognize each other as sovereign states for the first time. Travel between the GDR and Poland, Czechoslovakia, and Hungary becomes visa-free.

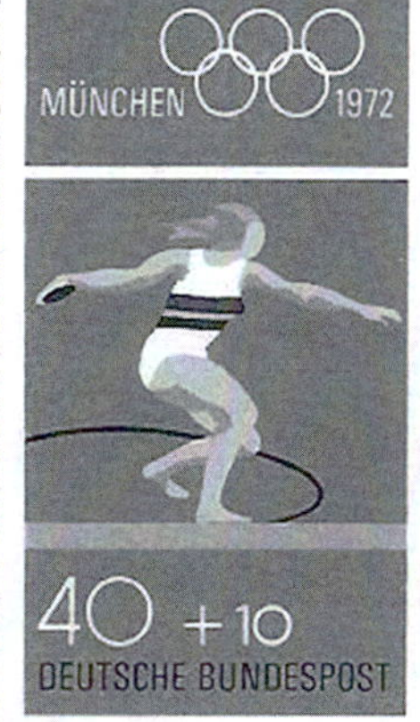

One of Polaroid's Focused Flash 400s made this difference. You can forget burnouts. You can forget blackouts. For shots as close as 3 ½ feet, a set of louvers closes down over the flashcube for beautiful exposures. For group shots as far as 10 feet away, they open wide to let out all the light from the Hi-Power flashcube. (Just shoot normally. It's automatic as you focus.) There are four models in our 400 Land camera line and prices start at under $60 without Focused Flash, under $70 with. Spend the extra $10 and see the light.

POLAROID®

Polaroid's Focused Flash 400s.

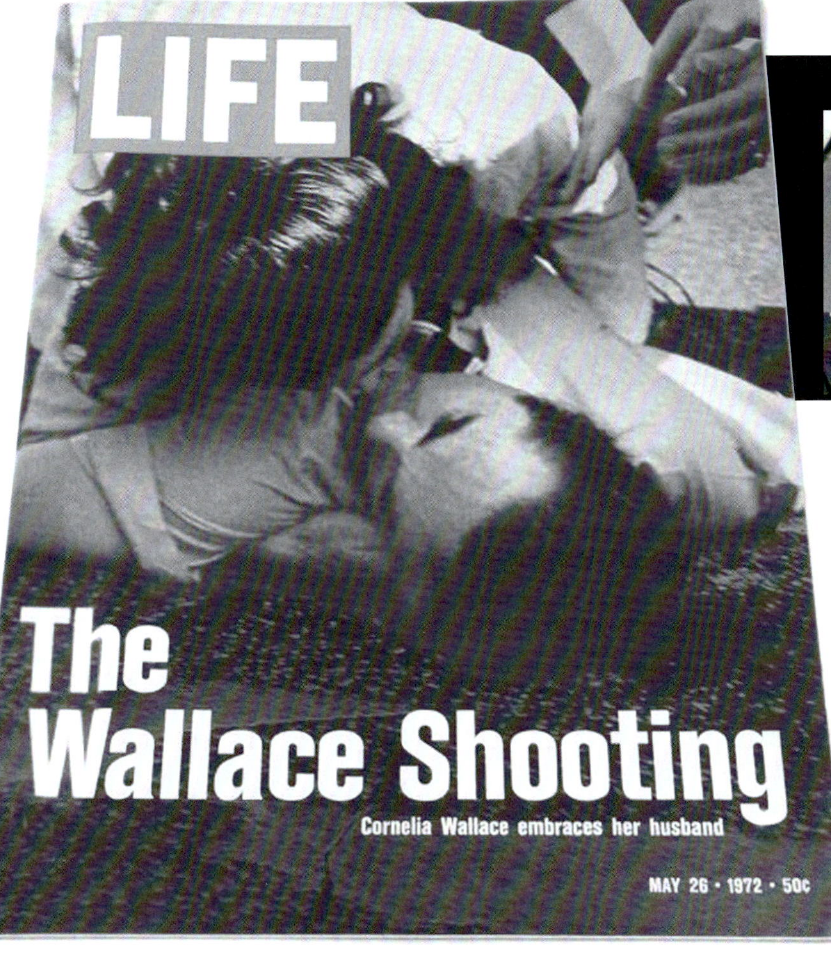

Wallace, Bremer

Segregationist Alabama Governor and presidential candidate **George C. Wallace** is shot five times by **Arthur Bremer** at a May 15th political rally in Maryland. The shooting leaves Wallace paralyzed from the waist down for the rest of his life. Bremer is sentenced to 63 years in prison.

In April, the U.S. and the Soviet Union join 70 nations in signing the Biological Weapons Convention, an agreement to ban biological warfare. And in May, **President Nixon** meets with Soviet leader **Leonid Brezhnev** in Moscow to sign the SALT I (Strategic Arms Limitation Talks) treaty and the Anti-Ballistic Missile Treaty.

The 33rd U.S. President, **HARRY S. TRUMAN**, passes away in Kansas City, Missouri at the age of 88. Truman utilized the Berlin Airlift and the Marshall Plan to rebuild post-war Western Europe and established NATO to contain communist expansion. He is survived by his wife, Bess.

The TUSKEGEE STUDY SCANDAL

Revelations by a whistleblower in 1972 bring to light the **Tuskegee Study of Untreated Syphilis**, an unethical clinical study conducted between 1932 and 1972 by the U.S. Public Health Service on African-American men with untreated syphilis in Macon County, Alabama. Subjects were told that told they were receiving free health care and that the study would last six months, but it actually lasted 40 years. None of the men were told that they had the disease, and none were treated. At the time of the revelation, syphilis had killed 28 participants, 100 died from related complications, and 40 spouses had been diagnosed with syphilis.

In 1997, President Bill Clinton formally apologizes on behalf of the United States to victims of the experiment.

Editorial cartoon by Lou Erikson, *Atlanta Constitution*, July 1972.

In the photo, African-American subjects have their blood sampled.

Civil Rights activist **Angela Davis** is released from a California jail in February. Held over a firearms purchase in connection with the kidnapping and murder of a Superior Court judge by proclaimed revolutionary Jonathan Jackson in 1970, Ms. Davis is bailed out by Fresno dairy farmer Rodger McAfee and found not guilty of murder in July. When the charges were originally filed, Davis became a fugitive listed on the FBI's Ten Most Wanted List.

Okinawa RETURN

Po...

Ph... ...nand Marcos

anno...

...e is placing the entire
...untry under martial law,
...ing the rising threats
...sed by violent student
...nonstrations, the
...mmunist Party, and the
...slim separatist move-
...nt. He orders the arrest
...pposition politicians in
...gress.

Marcos

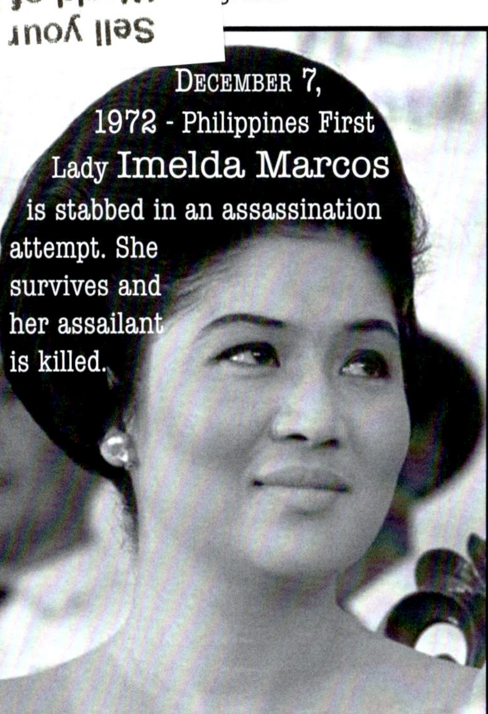

DECEMBER 7, 1972 - Philippines First Lady **Imelda Marcos** is stabbed in an assassination attempt. She survives and her assailant is killed.

Japan and the Government of the People's Republic of China sign an agreement on September 29th in Beijing, normalizing diplomatic relations after Japan breaks official ties with the Republic of China (Taiwan). And the Universal Postal Union decides to recognize the People's Republic of China as the only legitimate Chinese representative.

Mao Zedong by Edmund S. Valtman, Library of Congress

Okinawa is returned to Japan on May 15th, 1972. The United States occupied and governed the island for 27 years since the World War II Battle of Okinawa.

U.S. troops in Okinawa, 1945

Juan María Bordaberry is sworn in as President of **Uruguay** amid accusations of electoral fraud.

President of **Ecuador José María Velasco Ibarra** is deposed in a bloodless coup for the fifth time.

Marxist **Chilean** president **Salvador Allend**e forms a new government.

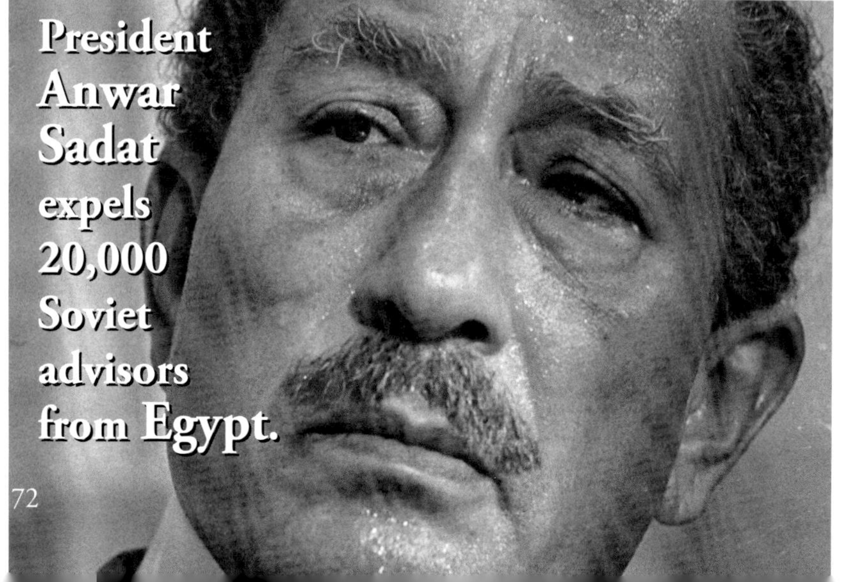

President **Anwar Sadat** expels 20,000 Soviet advisors from **Egypt**.

Iraq nationalizes the Iraq Petroleum Company.

BIRTH of *Bangladesh*

Bengali separatist fighters

The Bangladesh Liberation War commenced after military ruler **Agha Muhammad Yahya Khan** voided the 1971 election results in East Pakistan, forcing the government of Bangladesh to flee to India. The birth of Bangladesh was declared by the government in exile. The Indo-Pakistani War of 1971 launched on December 3rd with a massive invasion of East Pakistan by Indian forces. On December 16th, the Pakistani Army surrendered to the joint forces of India and the Bengali nationalist separatists, and the country of Bangladesh was officially established. On January 10, 1972, Independence leader **Sheikh Mujibur Rahman** returns to Bangladesh after spending over nine months in prison in Pakistan. He quickly declares a new constitutional government in Bangladesh, with himself as president.

Ceylon becomes **Sri Lanka** when its new constitution is ratified.

Flag of Sri Lanka

Following **King Mahendra's** death, 27-year-old **Birendra** succeeds his father to the throne of **Nepal**.

We'll take on any coffee in the house.

Compare the taste of Freeze-Dried Sanka® Brand Decaffeinated Coffee to any coffee you have in the house with or without caffein.
How can we make this challenge?
Because when we take out the caffein

we also take out a lot of the bitterness.
We leave you with a good, smooth-tasting cup of coffee.
Come on.
Put up your coffee.

GROUND ROAST COFFEE

FREEZE-DRIED
sanka
BRAND
97% CAFFEIN FREE
COFFEE

INSTANT COFFEE

INSTANT COFFEE

GROUND ROAST

FREEZE DRIED COFFEE

GF
GENERAL FOODS

In Canberra, the **Aboriginal Tent Embassy** is established as a permanent protest occupation site to call for political and land rights for Indigenous Australians. They present a list of demands to Parliament including territorial control, mining rights, preservation of sacred sites and compensation.

January 13 – Prime Minister of Ghana **Kofi Abrefa Busia** is overthrown in a military coup by Colonel **Ignatius Kutu Acheampong**.

August 16 – As part of a coup attempt, members of the Royal Moroccan Air Force fire upon **Hassan II** of Morocco's plane while he is traveling back to Rabat. The plane lands safely.

December 16 – In the ongoing Mozambican War of Independence, the Portuguese army kills 400 Africans in Tete, Mozambique. Portugal's wars against guerrilla fighters seeking independence in colonial African territories began in the early 1960s. Mozambique achieves independence in 1975.

Portuguese troops in Mozambique.

Dictator **Idi Amin** declares that Uganda will expel 50,000 Asians with British passports within 3 months.

Idi Amin by Edmund S. Valtman, Library of Congress

The great getaway machines.

Leave behind the regimented week that was,
to be continued another day.
Til then, get away
and sort things out
and be with friends on your Yamaha Enduros.
125cc and 175cc Enduros.
Light, quick, easy to handle,
yet, like all Yamaha dual-purpose machines,
they're built tough to take you off the road
and over the trails
leading back to quiet meadows and peaceful skies.
Yamaha Enduros.
The weekend getaway machines that have
earned the right to be called "Great."
See them at your Yamaha dealer.
Before next Saturday.

YAMAHA The great machines for '72.

People

Actor **Burt Reynolds** poses nude for the centerfold of the April, 1972 issue of *Cosmopolitan* magazine.

Comedian **George Carlin** is arrested in Milwaukee in July of 1972 for public obscenity when he recites his "Seven Words You Can Never Say On Television."

All-Star Pittsburgh Pirates baseball player

Roberto Clemente (38) dies in a plane crash while en route to deliver aid to Nicaraguan earthquake victims on December 31st.

Gloria Steinem and **Dorothy Pittman Hughes** co-found *Ms.*, the first feminist magazine.

Katherine Graham, above, becomes the first female Fortune 500 CEO in 1972, when she assumes the leadership of the ***Washington Post***. Graham became the *Post's* publisher in 1963 following the suicide of husband and publisher Philip Graham.

Gloria Steinem, left, & Dorothy Pittman Hughes

National Portrait Gallery, Smithsonian Institution

Under the leadership of U.S. Representative **Bella Abzug** of New York, the Equal Rights Amendment to prohibit discrimination on the basis of sex is passed by the U.S. House of Representatives and approved by the U.S. Senate in March 1972. It is sent to the states for ratification.

FBI HIRES WOMEN for the FIRST TIME

Joanne Pierce Misko walks with her male counterparts at the FBI Training Academy in 1972.

OFFICE OF THE DIRECTOR

UNITED STATES DEPARTMENT OF JUSTICE

FEDERAL BUREAU OF INVESTIGATION

WASHINGTON, D.C. 20535

FOR IMMEDIATE RELEASE
MAY 12, 1972

L. Patrick Gray, III, Acting Director, Federal Bureau of Investigation, today announced that women applicants will now be considered for the FBI Special Agent position.

Mr. Gray pointed out that this action is required by President Nixon's Executive Order 11478 dated August 9, 1969, relating to nondiscrimination and is further required by the recently enacted Equal Employment Opportunity Act of 1972 which was signed into law by President Nixon on March 24, 1972.

According to Mr. Gray the Special Agent applicant position before today has been limited to male citizens of the United States. All additional existing requirements for the Special Agent position will remain unchanged. The attached background sets forth in detail the Special Agent position requirements.

Acting FBI Director Gray said that the intensive 14-week Special Agent training course would remain unchanged. This course includes firearms training requiring the applicant to become qualified in the use of .38 caliber revolver, shotgun and rifle. The training period

While he ruled the FBI, Director J. Edgar Hoover forbade the hiring of women as Special Agents. But that changed following his death in 1972, enabling two women —**Joanne Pierce Misko** and **Susan Roley Malone** — to join 43 males at the FBI's Special Agent training course in Quantico, VA, in July 1972. 31-year-old Misko had been a nun in New York for 10 years before becoming an FBI researcher in 1970 while Malone, 25, previously served a stint in the U.S. Marine Corps.

The HUGHES HOAX

Irving, left, and Hughes

Author **Clifford Irving** announces in 1972 that he has co-written an authorized autobiography of infamous tycoon **Howard Hughes**. The obsesively reclusive billionaire, famed for his ground-breaking investments in flight and entertainment, doesn't immediately refute Irving's statement, enforcing the belief that Irving's account is authentic. But prior to the book's publication, Hughes denounces Irving and exposes the project as a hoax. A media sensation ensues, and Irving is convicted of fraud, spending 17 months in prison.

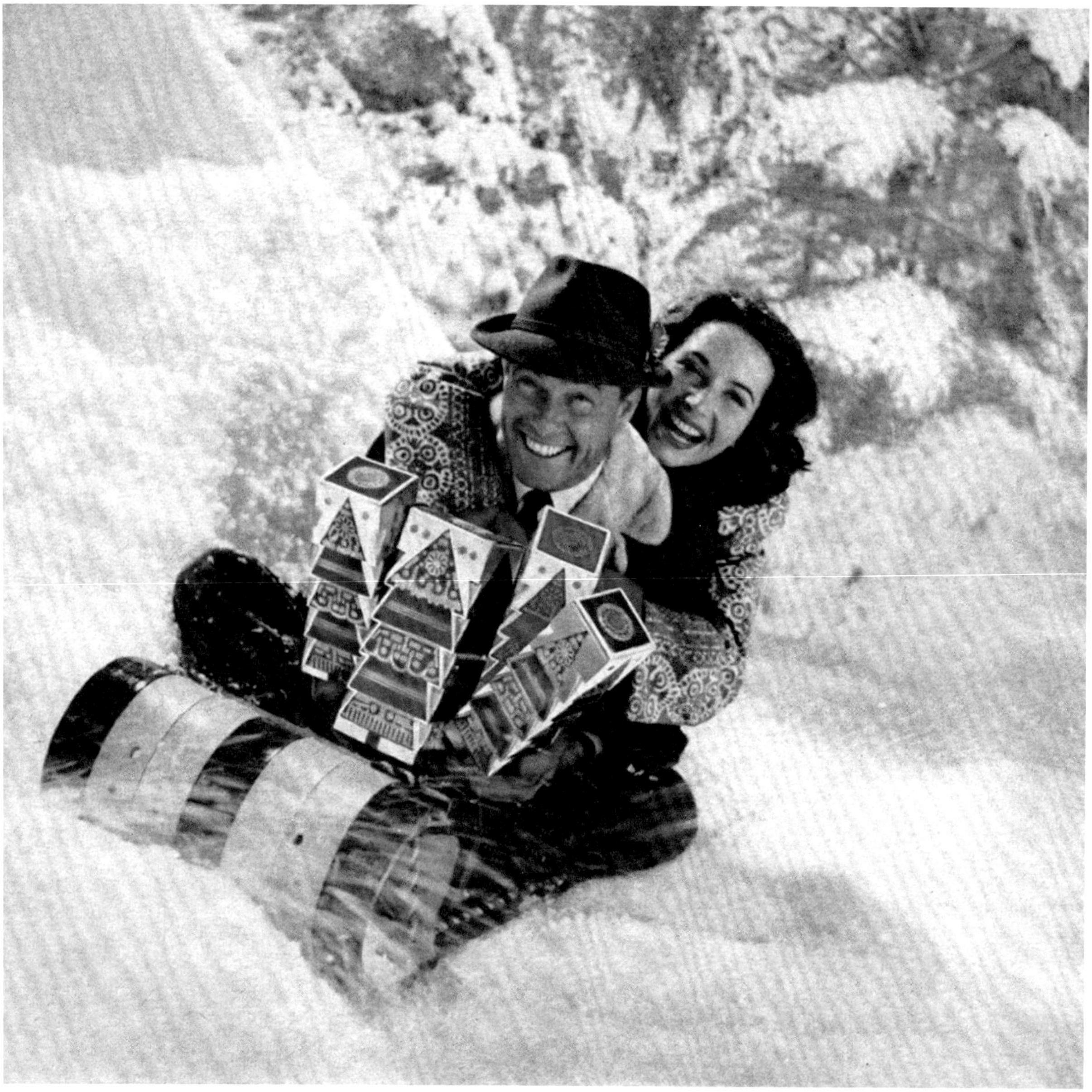

Here come happy holidays

Festively-wrapped Hiram Walker's Cordials... sure to be welcomed by everyone on your list

Give one, give all of these four popular favorites—flavorful Creme de Menthe, Creme de Cacao, Blackberry Flavored Brandy, and Anisette—and give them to one and all. Happily, you'll find they're beautifully packaged in foil at no extra cost. Your friends are sure to be flattered. And you'll feel like the smartest shopper yet.

CREME DE MENTHE, CREME DE CACAO, ANISETTE, 60 PROOF; BLACKBERRY FLAVORED BRANDY, 70 PROOF. HIRAM WALKER AND SONS, INC., PEORIA, ILLINOIS.

HIRAM WALKER'S

CORDIALS

A Rainbow of Distinctive Flavors

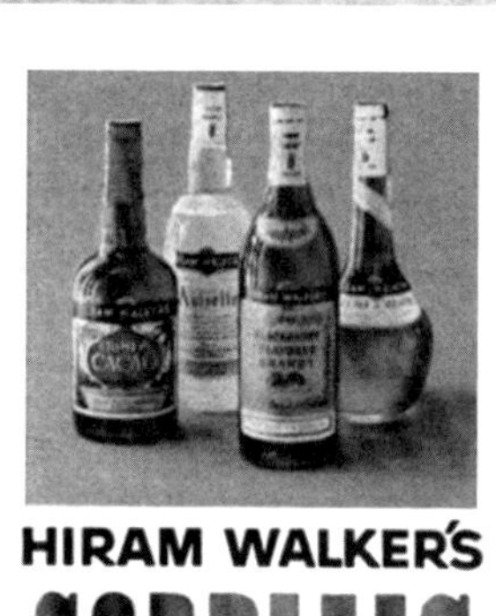

On November 24, 1971, a man calling himself **D. B. Cooper** and claiming to have a bomb, hijacked a Boeing 727 flying between Portland, Oregon, and Seattle, Washington. He demanded $200,000 and 4 parachutes, which he received upon landing in Tacoma, where all the passengers were released. With only 5 crew on board, the plane lifted off and — somewhere along the way — Cooper parachuted out.

In early 1972, teams of FBI agents aided by some 200 Army soldiers, along with Air Force personnel, National Guardsmen, and civilian volunteers, conduct a ground search lasting 36 days. A submarine plumbs the depths of Lake Merwin. A skeleton is discovered in an abandoned building, but it is identified as the remains of a teenaged girl who had been abducted and murdered several weeks earlier. The search and recovery operation uncover nothing significant related to the hijacking. D. B. Cooper is never located or identified. It remains the only unsolved case of air piracy in commercial aviation history.

Serbian flight attendant **Vesna Vulovi** is the only survivor of 28 passengers and crew when her plane crashes on January 26, 1972 in Czechoslovakia due to an exploding bomb.

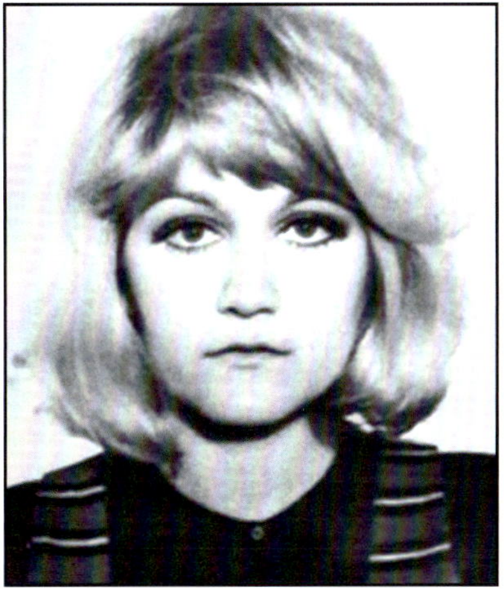

Vulovi is hospitalized in a coma with a fractured skull, three broken vertebrae, broken legs, broken ribs, and a fractured pelvis. But she makes an almost complete recovery, though left with a limp.

She holds the Guinness world record for surviving the highest fall without a parachute: 33,330 feet.

In January, 1972, **Yokoi Shichi** is discovered living in a cave in the jungles of Guam by two local fishermen. A sergeant in the Imperial Japanese Army during WWII, he had been in hiding almost 28 years after U.S. forces regained control of the island in 1944.

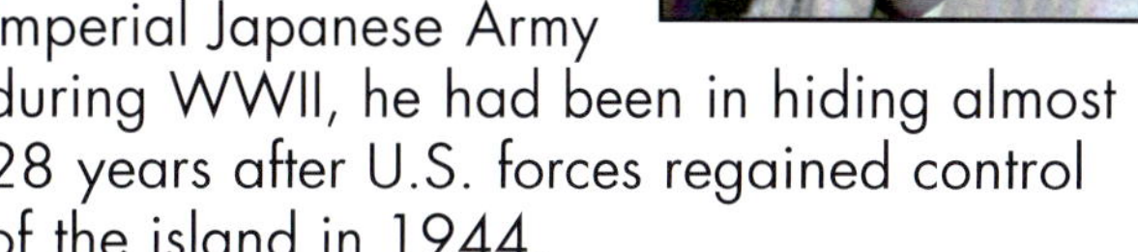

Yokoi knew in 1954 that the war was over. "It is with much embarrassment that I return," he says upon his return to Japan. "We Japanese soldiers were told to prefer death to the disgrace of getting captured alive."

Yokoi Shichi, above, and his cave.

ENQUIRING MINDS want to KNOW

midnight

VOL 19 — NO. 11　　SEPTEMBER 25, 1972　F　20¢

ONASSIS AIDE REVEALS:

Jackie's Fear Of Assassination Drives Ari Crazy

MEDICAL BREAKTHR...

NATIONAL ENQUIRER 20¢

How to Suppress Your Aggressions

JEANE DIXON:

...ssians Questioned Me to Learn If My ...wers Had Uncovered Soviet Secrets

Hollywood Is Talking About...

The Horrible Price Desi Arnaz Jr Must Pay For His Affair With Liza Minnelli

RESULTS OF ...SP SURVEY

DESI ARNAZ JR AND LIZA MINNELLI knew each other for years before their friendship blossomed into love

midnight

VOL. 18 — NO. 35　　MARCH 13, 1972　F　20¢

IQ Tests Can Wreck Your Child's Life

Leader Of A New Religion That Worships President Kennedy Says:

JFK IS BACK FROM THE DEAD

...His Spirit Is Among Us As The New Messiah

...z Taylor's Birthday Party　By Michael Caine

...Taylor shows off Richard Burton's gift, a fabulous ...ed pendant, at her 40th birthday celebration — a three-day blast in Budapest, Hungary. (Exclusive inside story by Michael Caine on back page.)

EXCLUSIVE Sophia Loren Pregnant Again

Producer Carlo Ponti beamed as he admitted for the first time — exclusively to The ENQUIRER — that his wife Sophia Loren is expecting her second child early next year. The couple, shown here during a visit to New York, are "in seventh heaven," Ponti said, "pray-ing for another healthy baby." (Interview on page 6.)

...QUIRER 20¢

How Pillow You Use Affects Your Sleep

Prominent Psychiatrists Explain...

HOWARD HUGHES HA... HIDING FOR 20 YEARS

...QUIRER 20¢

How You Can Tell If You're in Love

...rist Says They're Caught in the Middle...

...NTS HAVE BECOME ...TY'S SCAPEGOATS

NATIONAL ENQUIRER 20¢

How You Can Avoid Boredom

...Leading Psychics Reveal Their...

PREDICTIONS FOR 1972

...w Diet ...Popular ...he Stars
page 24

...our Hands ...About You
page 5

David Niven — 'When All I Wanted Was To Die'
page 11

4 Vital Qualities To Bring Success
page 31

Faith Healing Is Being Used in A California Hospital
page 6

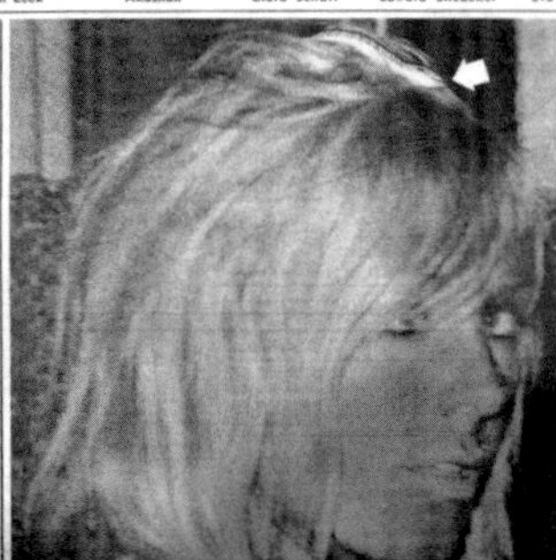

Warren Beatty: I'm Very Much in Love With Julie Christie

Tony Bennett: I'd Sacrifice My Wife and Baby for My Career

Singer Tony Bennett with bride Sandie and their daugh-ter, Joanna, 2, shown on arrival in London just after their wedding. Tony said: "Music is everything to me. It comes way ahead of everything else, even ahead of my family." Bennett tells of his bittersweet, cu... romance with Sandie in an interview on page 1...

Yoko Ono and John Lennon

Former Beatle and New York City residents **John Lennon** & wife **Yoko Ono** battle a U.S. Immigration Department deportation order, sparked by their participation in anti-war demonstrations. The Lennons are aided in their efforts to remain in the country by New York City Mayor **John Lindsay** and celebrities including **Bob Dylan**. Their fight lasts until 1975, when the deportation order is overturned.

Wedding day, Las Vegas, 1967

Elvis Presley and his wife, **Priscilla**, separate in February and file for divorce in August. Originally married in Las Vegas in 1967, both maintained extra-marital affairs.

Star Trek fans are delighted when the first Star Trek convention takes place in New York City's Statler Hilton Hotel.

HOW TO GET MORE VACATION FOR YOUR MONEY.

TWA's GETAWAY PROGRAM FOR 1972.

WE HELP YOU PLAN.
Send us the card and we'll send you back our free Getaway* Kit. It's got 2 pounds of books and brochures to help you plan your own perfect vacation. It tells you where to go. When's the best time to go. What it will cost. How to qualify for bargain fares. And all sorts of other helpful things. (If the card's gone, send to TWA, P.O. Box 303, Farmingdale, N.Y. 11735.)

WE HELP YOU SAVE.
Our Getaway Guidebooks are the biggest sellers in the business. No wonder. For only $1 apiece, they help you find the best hotels, restaurants, shops, etc. Then get you discounts on everything.

WE HELP YOU PAY.
Besides more vacation for your money, we also give you more money for your vacation. Our Getaway Card requires no minimum income, and asks no yearly fee. With one, you can charge airfare, hotels, meals, cars, etc. Then take up to two years to pay.

*Getaway is a service mark owned exclusively by TWA.

BRITISH ROYAL CHRONICLES

1400 parading soldiers, 200 horses and 400 musicians come together outside Buckingham Palace in a display of military precision called Trooping of the Colour. **Queen Elizabeth II** here explains the ceremony to her youngest son, **Prince Edward**.

The Queen and **Prince Philip, Duke of Edinburgh** celebrate their twenty-five year Silver Wedding Anniversary in the Belgian suite in Buckingham Palace, London.

Prince Charles, Prince Edward, Queen Elizabeth II, the Duke of Edinburgh, Prince Andrew, and **Princess Anne** pose for a group portrait at Buckingham Palace.

In 1972, the Queen orders a 90-minute 1969 BBC film called *Royal Family* to be locked away, apparently over fears it will destroy the royal mystique. More than 30 million people viewed the "fly-on-the-wall" private life documentary when it originally aired in 1969. The Queen regretted her initial decision to allow the film and is believed to have said the film was "killing the monarchy."

Scenes from the film

NOT CROSS CRIME SCENE D

John Wojtowicz

John Wojtowicz, 27, and **Sal Naturile**, 18, hold seven Chase Manhattan Bank employees hostage for 14 hours in August during a failed bank robbery attempt in Brooklyn, N.Y. By some accounts, Wojtowicz wanted money to pay for his sex reassignment surgery. The caper would be the basis for the 1975 film, DOG DAY AFTERNOON, starring **Al Pacino**.

In March, a gang uses dynamite to blast a hole in the concrete roof of the United California Bank in Laguna Niguel, CA, making off with $9 million from safe deposit boxes in the vault. The crew of professional burglars is led by **Amil Dinsio** and includes his brother, nephews and brother-in-law. A previous burglary and airline logs lead police to the perpretators, all of whom are arrested and convicted.

On January 2, 1972, a group of men enter New York's Pierre Hotel with a room reservation and proceed to round up staff at gunpoint. The robbers, including **Samuel Nalo** and mobster **Robert "Bobby" Comfort**, wear wigs and fake nose disguises. They lift $4 million in jewelery from safe deposit boxes held downstairs in bank vaults. Before departing, they tip each staff hostage $20.

The robbers, who had previously stolen $1,000,000 in jewelry and cash from **Sophia Loren's** suite in the Sherry Netherland Hotel, are later apprehended based on information provided by a mob informant. The Pierre caper would be listed in the **Guinness Book of World Records** as the largest hotel robbery in history.

Gacy as Pogo the Clown

One of the most infamous serial killers in criminal history, **John Wayne Gacy** (b. 1942) commences his six-year stretch of horrifying murders in 1972. Known as the "Killer Clown" because he performs at children's events as "Pogo the Clown" or "Patches the Clown," Gacy lures young men or boys into his home, where he handcuffs, rapes and tortures them before murdering them by asphyxiation. He then buries them in the crawlspace beneath his suburban Chicago house or dumps them in the the Des Plaines River. Eventually convicted of 33 murders in 1980, he would be executed in 1994. An unrepentent sociopath, his final spoken words were reported to be "kiss my ass."

The **Alphabet Murders** (also known as the Double Initial Murders) are an unsolved series of child murders which occured between 1971 and 1973 in Rochester, New York. All three victims of the Alphabet Murders are girls aged ten or eleven, whose surname begins with the same letter as that of her first name. Each victim has been sexually assaulted and murdered by strangulation before her body is discarded in or near a town also beginning with same letter as her initials.

Artist's rendering of an unknown individual seen with victim Michelle Maenza prior to her murder.

Rodney **James Alcala** recommenced a rape and muder spree spanning the country and including at least 8 victims between 1971 and 1979, though the true victim count remains unknown, and could be much higher. Alcala compiled a collection of more than 1,000 photographs of women and teenage girls, many in sexually explicit poses. He tortured his victims before raping and strangling them. He is known as the **Dating Game Killer** because of his 1978 appearance on that television game show in the midst of his murder spree. (The bachelorette refused their date, calling him "creepy.")

Alcala is arrested in late 1979 and ultimately sentenced to death in California and 25 years to life in New York. He will die in prison in 2021 at the age of 77.

Alcala

Kraft sentenced to death in 1989

Variously known as the **Scorecard Killer**, for coded lists he kept, the **Southern California Strangler,** and the **Freeway Killer**, **Randy Kraft** is believed to have raped, tortured and killed a total of 67 victims. between 1971 and 1983. His victims were males between the ages of 13 through their twenties. Many of his victims had been US Marines and most had high levels of alcohol and tranquilizers in their blood systems.

He is ultimately charged with and convicted of sixteen homicides. As of 2021, he remains incarcerated on death row at San Quentin State Prison, California.

1972 ADVERTISEMENT

Effective January 10, 1972, you can pay for your trip on Amtrak trains with a credit card in 63 cities across the United States. With more to be added in the future.

This marks the first time that a unified credit card system applies to the nation's intercity rail passenger network.

Amtrak will accept American Express, Master Charge and the Rail Travel Card.

We're pleased that Amtrak can now offer you the two surest ingredients for a pleasant trip. Trains and credit.

We're making the trains worth traveling again.

Amtrak

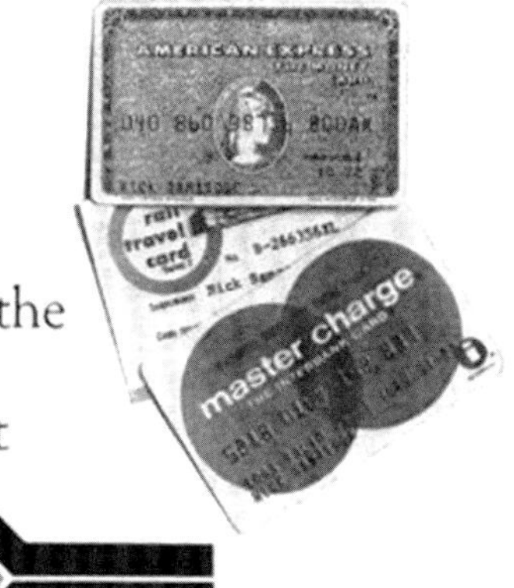

YOU TAKE OUR TRAINS WE TAKE YOUR CREDIT CARDS

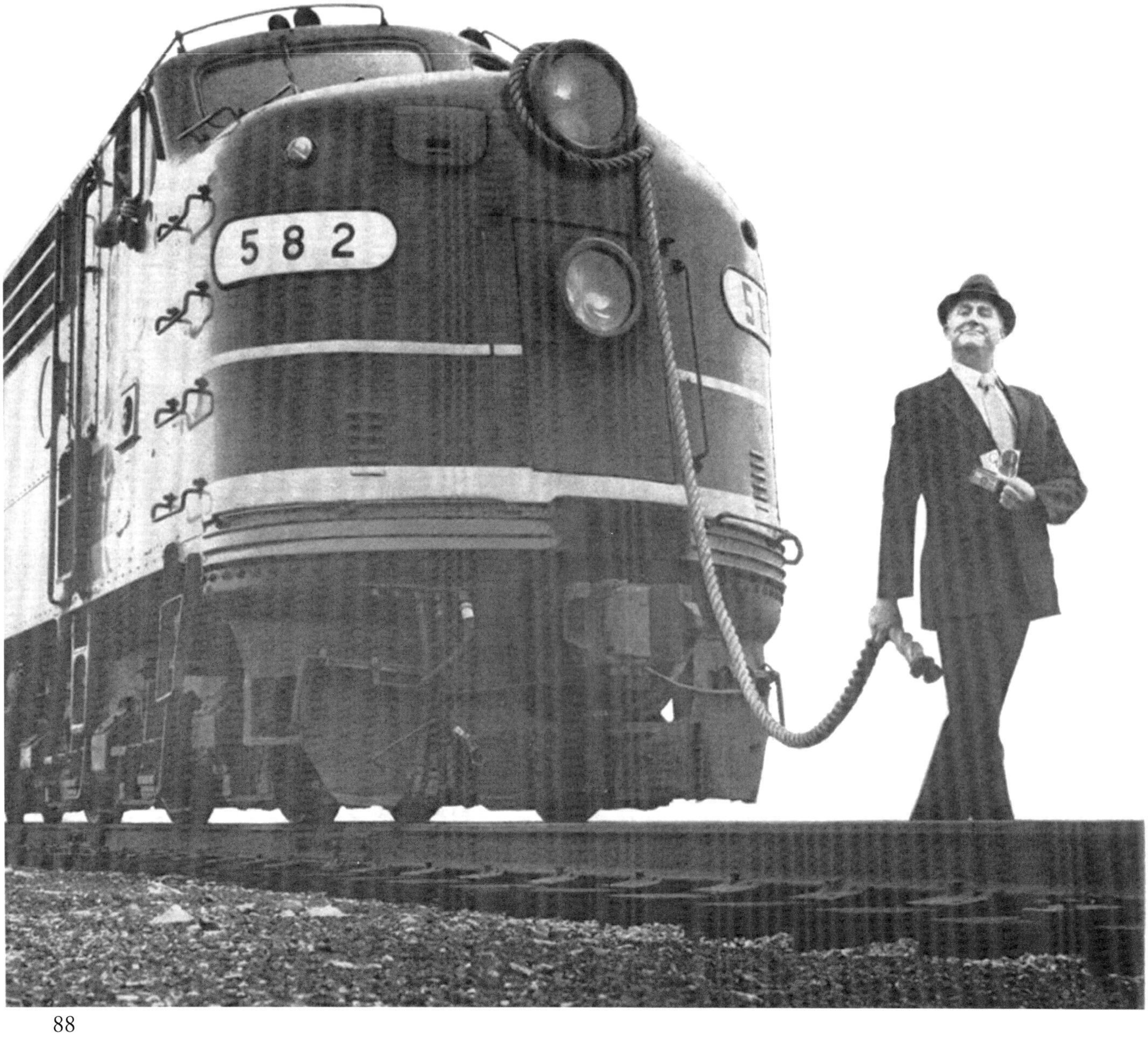

famous births

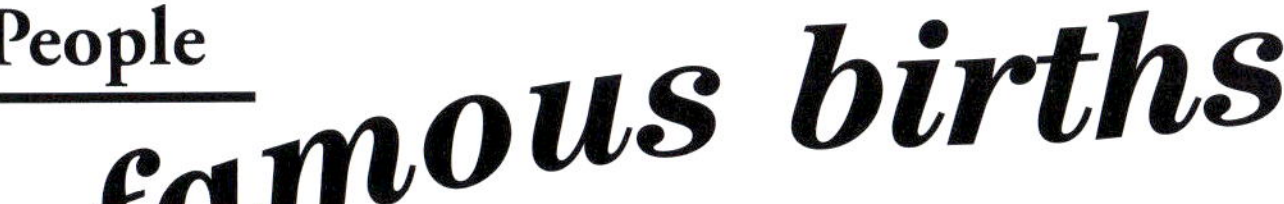

QUEEN
Letizia
of the **Spain**

Amy Coney Barrett

Beto O'Rourke

Nikki Haley

Mary
Crown Princess of Denmark

MOST ADMIRED MAN — **Richard M. Nixon**
U.S. President

MOST ADMIRED WOMAN — **Pat Nixon**
First Lady

Pat
Nixon

Passings

J. EDGAR HOOVER, 77 - The first director of the FBI from its inception in 1924 until his death. Instrumental in building the organization, he later became controversial for secretive abuses of power.

Hoover

ADAM CLAYTON POWELL JR., 63 - Serving 26 years in the U.S. House of Representatives, he was the first African American to be elected to Congress from New York.

CHARLES ATLAS, 80 - Bodybuilder and exercise program marketer.

LOUIS LEAKEY, 60 - Famed paleontologist.

EDWARD VIII, the Duke of Windsor, 77.

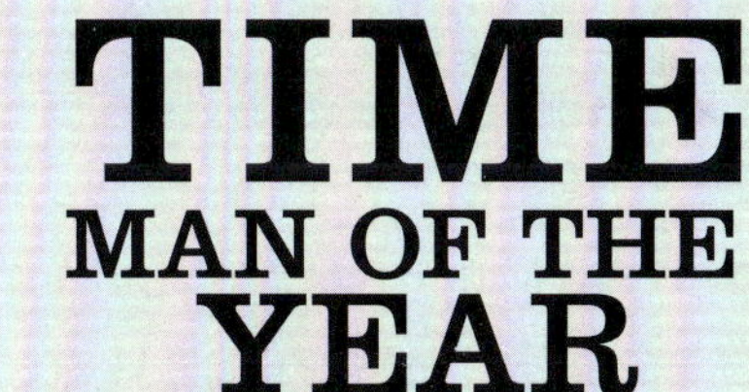

Richard M. Nixon

Why Opel is a good buy in today's market.

Opel's price.

Buick's Opel 1900's are among the lowest priced cars in the country. (Now that the surcharge and excise tax have been repealed, they're an even better buy.) And when you consider the things you get for your money, the price seems even lower. Big things like a quiet 1.9 liter engine, rack and pinion steering, contoured bucket seats, nylon carpeting and power front disc brakes. Little things like a light that tells you your brake system is working. And one that tells you when your clutch needs adjustment. Things that aren't included in the price of a lot of small cars. That's why Opel prices are some of the best values around.

Opel's reputation.

People who know cars have said a lot of nice things about the 1972 Opels. For example, CAR AND DRIVER magazine said, "Given our choice of any super-coupe between the Atlantic and the Pacific, we'd take the Opel Rallye," and rated the Opel Rallye ahead of the five other competitive cars they tested. ROAD AND TRACK tested the Rallye against two other competitive cars and also rated it tops. Do your own test drive at your nearest Buick/Opel dealer's. We think you'll have a lot of nice things to say about the 1972 Opels yourself.

Opel's service network.

A lot of people have small cars they just can't seem to get service for. Opel is serviced by more than 2,200 Buick/Opel dealers from coast to coast. So you won't have to go very far when you need service or maintenance. Fortunately, though, Opels are designed not to need service and maintenance too often . . . with features like automatic exhaust valve rotators for long engine life and a really heavy-duty cooling system.

Opel's car.

There's a long list of standard features that we think help make Opel a better value than other small cars. But no list could tell you what really makes Opel different. You'll have to take a trip to your Buick/Opel dealer's. One test drive will tell you all you need to know.

Opel 1900 Sport Coupe

Buick's Opel. Still a small price. Still a big value.

Public perceptions of DDT changed drastically from the 1940s to the '60s.

Following seven months of hearings in 1971 and 1972, the Environmental Protection Agency (EPA) bans most uses of the pesticide DDT. DDT and other pesticides have been shown to cause cancer and their agricultural use is a threat to the environment and to wildlife, particularly birds.

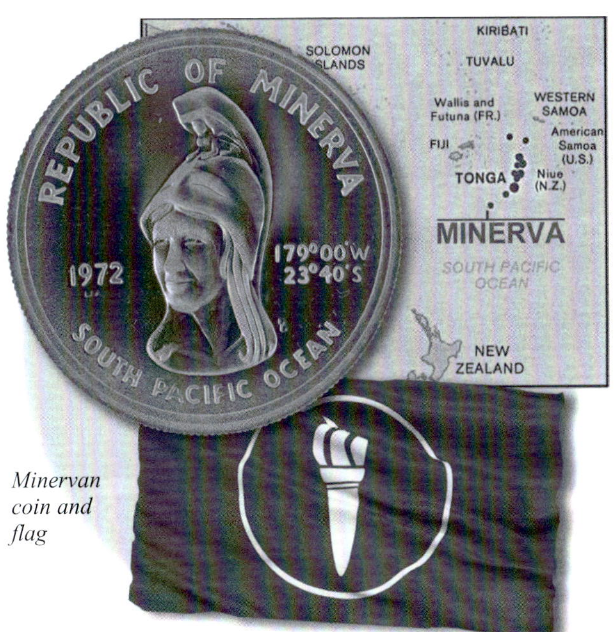

Minervan coin and flag

Las Vegas real estate developer and political activist **Michael Oliver** establishes a sovereign micronation in 1972 called the **Republic of Minerva** on reefs off the Polynesian archipelago country, Tonga. Oliver envisions a libertarian society with "no taxation, welfare, subsidies, or any form of economic interventionism." Tonga soon dismantles the attempt by annexing the reef.

The "tea house" **Mellow Yellow** opens in the Weesperzijde neighborhood of Amsterdam, discreetly offering pot to smoke or take out and pioneering the legal sale of cannabis in the Netherlands. The shop takes its name from a Donovan song about baked bananas.

Another Skyjacker Shot

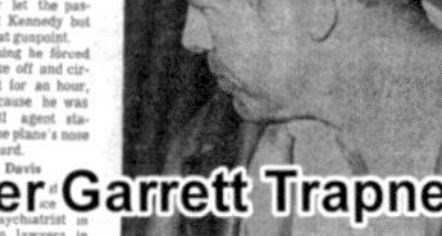

NEW YORK — (UPI) — A shady adventurer with history of mental illness pulled a gun from an arm cast yesterday to hijack a TWA jetliner and held it for nine hours until was shot by an FBI agent posing as a member of the crew.

The hijacker, identified as Garrett Brock Trapnell, 34, Miami, had demanded to be flown from Kennedy International Airport in Dallas to pick up a prisoner in the county there and then on to Europe.

He missed gun in hand at the boarding ramp as waited for a fresh TWA to climb to the cockpit, himself relaxed his guard a moment.

An FBI marksman manning as a crew member of two shots, hitting Trapnell in the left shoulder and arm and ending the nine-hour seige.

It was the second hijacker in three days. The first dish Thursday chinnequse, N.J. he tried to fly ,000 ransom.

Record

appell, a native of Wal-, Mass., who has faced inal charges at at least states, Canada and the plane, on a flight from Los Angeles to New York

The hijacker let the passengers off at Kennedy but held the crew at gunpoint.

At mid-morning he forced the pilot to take off and circle the airport for an hour, apparently because he was afraid an FBI agent stationed under the plane's nose would try to board.

ela Davis, at a psychiatrist in Miami.

He demanded Angela Davis' release from prison, a personal talk with President Nixon and $306,000.

Hijacker Garrett Trapnell

GARRETT TRAPNELL — CAPTURED SKYJACKER
Photo after he escaped from hospital in 1971

Israeli soldiers rescuing hostages on Sabena Flight 571

June 3 Hijackers Willie Roger Holder & girl-friend Catherine Kerkow

June 23 Hijacker Martin McNally

July 31 Hijacker George Wright

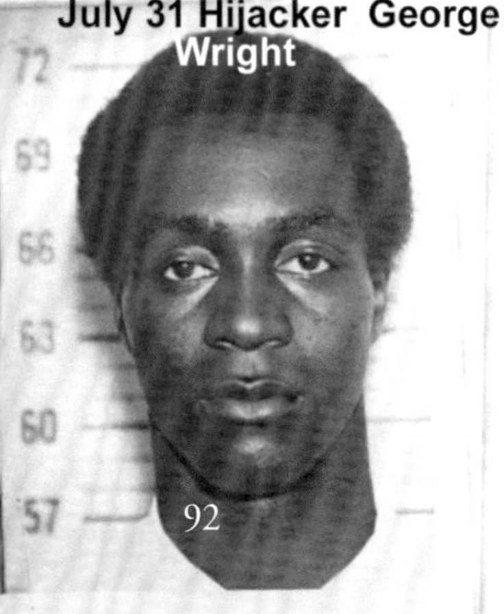

Skyjacking:
THE NEW NORMAL

A PARTIAL LISTING of 1972 EVENTS

January 28 • Con man and bank robber Garrett Trapnell hijacks LA to NY TWA Flight 2, demanding $306,800, the release of activist Angela Davis, and Presidential clemency. Trapnell is shot, wounded & arrested by the FBI at Kennedy Airport.

April 7 • United Airlines Flight 855, Newark to LA, with 85 passengers and a crew of six, is hijacked by Richard McCoy Jr. during a stopover in Denver. He demands and obtains a $500,000 cash ransom, but is arrested two days after the hijacking.

May 5 • Frederick Hahneman hijacks Eastern AirLines Flight 175, Allentown, PA, to Miami, FL. After receiving $303,000, he orders the pilot to fly to Honduras, where he parachutes out. Following a manhunt, he eventually surrenders.

May 8 • Sabena Flight 571, Brussels to Lod, is hijacked by 4 members of the Palestinian Black September terrorist group, who demand that Israel release Palestinian prisoners in exchange for the hostages. The hijackers are all killed or captured by Israeli commandos.

May 24 • South African Airways Flight 727 is hijacked near Johannesburg and flown to Malawi. The crew and passengers escape, and the hijackers surrender to Malawian security forces.

June 3 • Western Airlines Flight 701 LA to Seattle is hijacked by Vietnam veteran Willie Roger Holder & his girl-friend, who claim to have a bomb. 97 passengers deplane in San Francisco, and the hijackers are given $500,000. The plane flies to Algeria where the hijackers are granted political asylum, though the ransom is returned.

June 8 • Seven men and three women hijack a plane from Czechoslovakia to West Germany.

June 23 • Martin J. McNally aka Robert W. Wilson hijacks American Airlines Flight 119, demanding $502,500. In St. Louis, a businessman, hearing news reports about the hijacking, crashes his Cadillac into the taxiing plane. The hijacker transfers to a new plane and jumps out over Indiana. He is eventually captured & the loot recovered.

July 2 • Pan Am Flight 841, San Francisco to Saigon, is hijacked by a South Vietnamese man as a protest against US involvement in the Vietnam War. The captain and passengers overcome and kill hijacker after the plane lands in Saigon.

July 5 • Two Bulgarian immigrants hijack Pacific Southwest Airlines Flight 710 after take-off from Sacramento demanding $800,000 and to be flown to the Soviet Union. The hijacking ends in San Francisco when FBI agents storm the plane killing both hijackers and one passenger.

July 31 • Delta Air Lines Flight 841 from Detroit to Miami is hijacked by five members of the Black Liberation Army including George Wright. The hijackers exchange the passengers for $1 million and force the plane to fly to Algeria, where the plane and cash are returned but the hijackers released.

September 15 • Three armed Croatians hijack Scandinavian Airlines Flight 130, ordering it to land in, Malmö, Sweden. 90 passengers and 4 crew are released in exchange for 500,000 Swedish Kronor and seven Croatians imprisoned in Sweden. The plane then flies to Madrid where the hijackers are arrested.

October 29 • Lufthansa Flight 615 from Beirut to Frankfurt, is hijacked by three men and flown to Zagreb, where they demand the release of the 3 surviving Munich Massacre perpetrators. After boarding the three men, the plane flies to Tripoli in Libya where all hostages are released.

November 10 • Southern Airways Flight 49 is hijacked by three men who threaten to fly the plane into a nuclear reactor unless they are given $10 million in cash. The hijacking ends when the plane lands on a foam-covered runway in Havana, Cuba, and the men are captured after attempting to escape.

December 14 • Larry Maxwell Stanford hijacks Quebecair Flight 321 en route to Toronto. The plane diverts to Montreal where the hijacker surrenders.

Carving is completed on March 3rd on the rock relief Confederate memorial at Stone Mountain, Georgia. Depicting Confederacy President **Jefferson Davis** and Generals **Robert E. Lee** and **Stonewall Jackson** on horseback, it is the largest bas-relief artwork in the world at 90 feet high and 190 feet wide. The monument will increasingly draw criticism for it's commemoration and celebration of an unrecognized breakaway state which fought against the United States of America in order to validate and continue the enslavement of Black people and oppose emancipation. The NAACP has dubbed the Stone Mountain monument "...the largest shrine to white supremacy in the history of the world."

On July 10, 1972, elephants crazed by heat and drought in India's Chandka Forest stampede five villages, killing at least 24 people. Today, the area is an elephant sanctuary.

In New Delhi, India, nearly 100 people die after drinking bootlegged liquor at a January 21st wedding party. The deaths are caused by methyl, or "wood," alcohol sold as a substitute for whisky to laborers celebrating the wedding.

Police trace the drink to a man suspected of being a major bootlegger. They find him, his mother and his brother dead among the wedding guests after drinking their own product.

February 18 – The California Supreme Court voids the state's death penalty, commuting all death sentences to life in prison.

June 29 – The Supreme Court of the United States rules that capital punishment is unconstitutional in Furman v. Georgia.

October 30 – U.S. President Richard Nixon approves legislation to increase Social Security spending by $5.3 billion.

December 15 – The Commonwealth of Australia ordains equal pay for women.

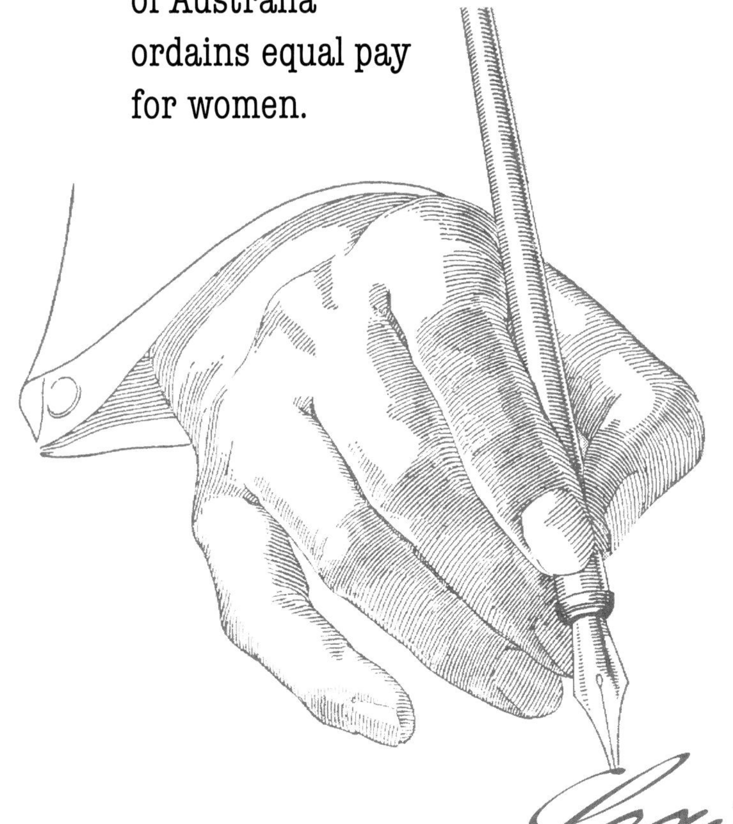

Do you hear me loud and clear?

Is your loving family taking you for granted? And, just because you fill the role of homemaker so superbly, don't they realize that your training really qualifies you for much better things? Express your (slightly rebellious) personality with this Apron/Potholder Set. The important question is hand-screened on heavy green/white 100% cotton, with adjustable chrome buckle to fit all sizes of women's libbers.

haverhill's

A Subsidiary of Time Inc.

Legislation

AROUND THE WORLD

The world population increases by more than 2% to 3.85 billion in 1972. The U.S. population climbs to over 209 million.

1972 is the longest year ever, as two leap seconds are added during this 366-day year, an event which has not been repeated since. For the first and last time, a 2nd leap second is added (23:59:60) to a year, making 1972 366 days and two seconds long, the longest year ever within the context of Coordinated Universal Time (UTC).

Green   *Shaefer*   *Wells*

DISASTERS

The **Managua Earthquake**

December 23 -- A magnitude 6.2 earthquake near the Nicaraguan capital of Managua kills up to 11,000 people. The problems are compounded when Nicaraguan President **Anastasio Somoza** is accused of misappropriating millions of dollars in foreign aid.

A **6.7 magnitude earthquake** shatters southern **Iran**, killing over **5,300 people** in the Fars province on April 10th.

Aftermath of Hurricane Agnes in Richmond, VA

On June 9th, 15" of rain concentrated in a small area leads to the **Black Hills flood**, killing 238 in South Dakota. And **Hurricane Agnes** hits the U.S. East Coast in mid-June, killing 128 people and causing $2.1 billion in damage, a record for the time.

Wreck of the RMS Queen Elizabeth

January 9 – **The RMS Queen Elizabeth is destroyed** by a fire in Hong Kong harbor.

February 26 – **A coal sludge spill** kills 125 people in Buffalo Creek, West Virginia.

March 26 – **An avalanche on Mount Fuji** kills 19 climbers.

May 13 – **A nightclub fire** atop the Sennichi department store in Osaka, Japan, kills 115.

June 16 – **108 die** as two passenger trains hit the debris of a collapsed railway tunnel near Soissons, France.

June 18 – **Flooding, building collapses** and landslides kill over 150 people in Hong Kong's worst flooding in recorded history.

October 6 – **A train crash** in Saltillo, Mexico kills 208 people.

Oct 30 – **A commuter train collision** in Chicago kills 45 and injures hundreds.

Hong Kong building collapse due to flooding

AIRLINE DISASTERS

January 7 - Iberia Airlines Flight 602 crashes into a mountain peak on the island of Ibiza, killing 104.

May 5 - An Alitalia DC-8 crashes west of Palermo, Sicily. 115 die.

June 18 - 118 are killed when a Trident 1 airliner crashes shortly after takeoff from London Heathrow Airport.

August 14 - 156 die when an East German Ilyushin airliner crashes near East Berlin.

October 13 - Uruguayan Flight 571, transporting a rugby team, crashes in the Andes mountains near the Argentina/Chile border. Sixteen are found alive in December, but they have had to resort to cannibalism to survive.

October 16 - A plane carrying Louisiana Congressman Hale Boggs and three others vanishes in Alaska. The wreckage is never been found.

December 8 - United Airlines Flight 553 crashes during an aborted landing in Chicago, killing 45 passengers, including Congressman George Collins, CBS News correspondent Michele Clark and Dorothy Hunt, wife of Watergate conspirator E. Howard Hunt.

December 29 - Eastern Air Lines Flight 401 crashes into the Florida Everglades, killing 101 of 176 on board.

THE "BRAIN" THAT FITS IN YOUR SHIRT POCKET

Our Bowmar/901B Electronic Calculator is so compact it actually fits in your shirt pocket. Compare its size (3x5x1") and weight (less than a pocket transistor radio) with that of other so-called "pocket models," which often measure 8" or more and weigh two or three pounds.

But size and weight are only part of the story. **The Bowmar/901B** performs every arithmetical function you would expect from an electronic desk calculator and some found only in advanced models. There are such niceties as
- stored constant
- full floating decimal
- chain multiplication and division.

The Bowmar/901B features
- 8-digit read-out
- the advanced technology of LIC circuitry.
- It's powered by contained NiCd rechargeable batteries (charger is included)
- but it can be operated directly from house current if desired.

As an executive, salesman, accountant, engineer or student—anyone who needs fast answers, you can hardly operate competitively without the aid of an electronic calculator. It has become the indispensable tool. But until now, price has been a hurdle. And here, beyond size and performance, is the best surprise: **US-made Bowmar/901B costs just $179**—less than you would expect to pay for a mechanical calculator.

Order the Bowmar/901B in confidence. Use it for two weeks. Then—if it doesn't fill your every expectation, return it for full refund. There will be no quibbling. You are the only judge. But, we know this won't happen. The speed, compactness and convenience of the **Bowmar/901B** give you an advantage—a competitive edge you'll simply not want to do without.

☐ **Please send me the Bowmar/901B** with carry case, battery charger, operating instructions and warranty. My check for $180 ($179 plus $1 postage and insurance) is enclosed. California residents add tax. I may return the unit within two weeks for full refund if not satisfied.

Name________________________________

Address_____________________________

______________________________ Zip________

What's New

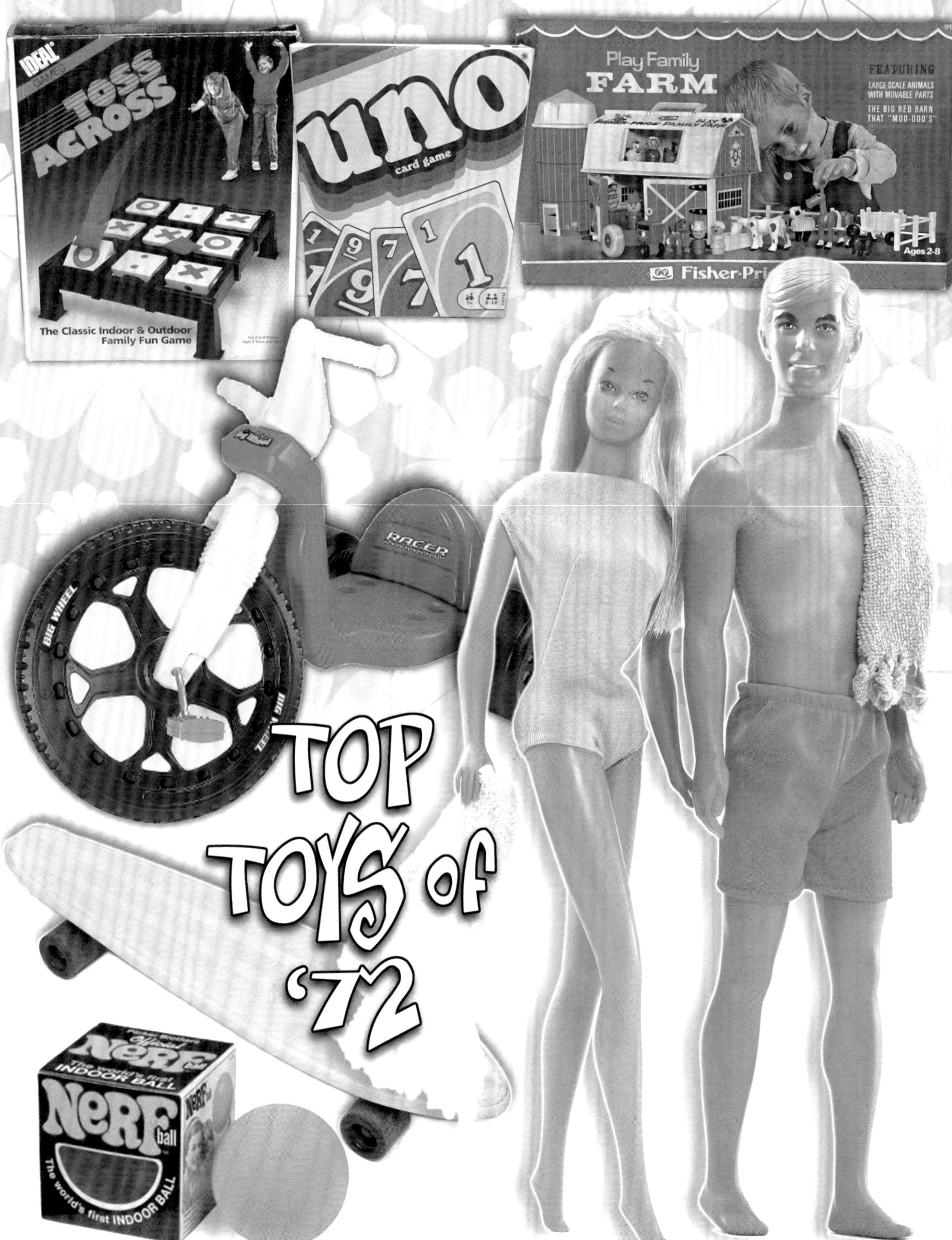
IDEAL
GAMES
TOSS ACROSS
The Classic Indoor & Outdoor
Family Fun Game
UNO
card game
Play Family
FARM
FEATURING
LARGE SCALE ANIMALS
WITH MOVABLE PARTS
THE BIG RED BARN
THAT "MOO-OOO'S"
Ages 2-8
Fisher-Price
BIG WHEEL
RACER
TOP TOYS of '72
NERF ball
The world's first INDOOR BALL

New PRODUCTS And INVENTIONS

The video game age dawns when the **Magnavox Odyssey**, the first commercial home video game system, goes on sale to the public.

Nolan Bushnell and **Ted Dabney** co-found **Atari** and launch their seminal arcade version of **Pong**, the first video game to achieve commercial success.

Hewlett-Packard's HP-35

is the first commercially-available scientific pocket calculator. Price: $395.

Video Cassette Recording (VCR) is a

new analog recording format first launched by Philips. VCRs use large 2-reel cassettes with half-inch wide magnetic tape. Three playing times are available: 30, 45 and 60 minutes.

The **Country Bear Jamboree** is a popular new attraction in the Magic Kingdom at Florida's Walt Disney World. The stage show features audio-animatronic bear characters performing country music.

McDonald's introduces the **Egg McMuffin**.

NEW BRANDS

Snapple

Mr. Coffee

Eggbeaters

Nutrisystem

Stove Top Stuffing

The first **POPEYES** fried chicken restaurant opens in New Orleans as "Chicken on the Run." Several months later, proprietor Alvin C. Copeland re-names the place "Popeyes."

1972 *Motor Trend* Car of the Year:

Citroen SM

HOTTEST MUSCLE CARS *of* 1972

Buick GS 455 Stage 1
Oldsmobile 4-4-2 W-30
Chevrolet Camaro Z28
Pontiac GTO 455HO
Chevrolet Chevelle SS 454
Ford Mustang 351 HO

Buick GS 455

• CARS INTRODUCED IN 1972 •

HONDA CIVIC

MERCEDES-BENZ S-CLASS

The Joy of Sex is published. British author Alex Comfort's illustrated "how-to" sex manual is a bestseller, spending 11 weeks atop the *New York Times* list and over a year in the top five.

NEWS *The Latest*

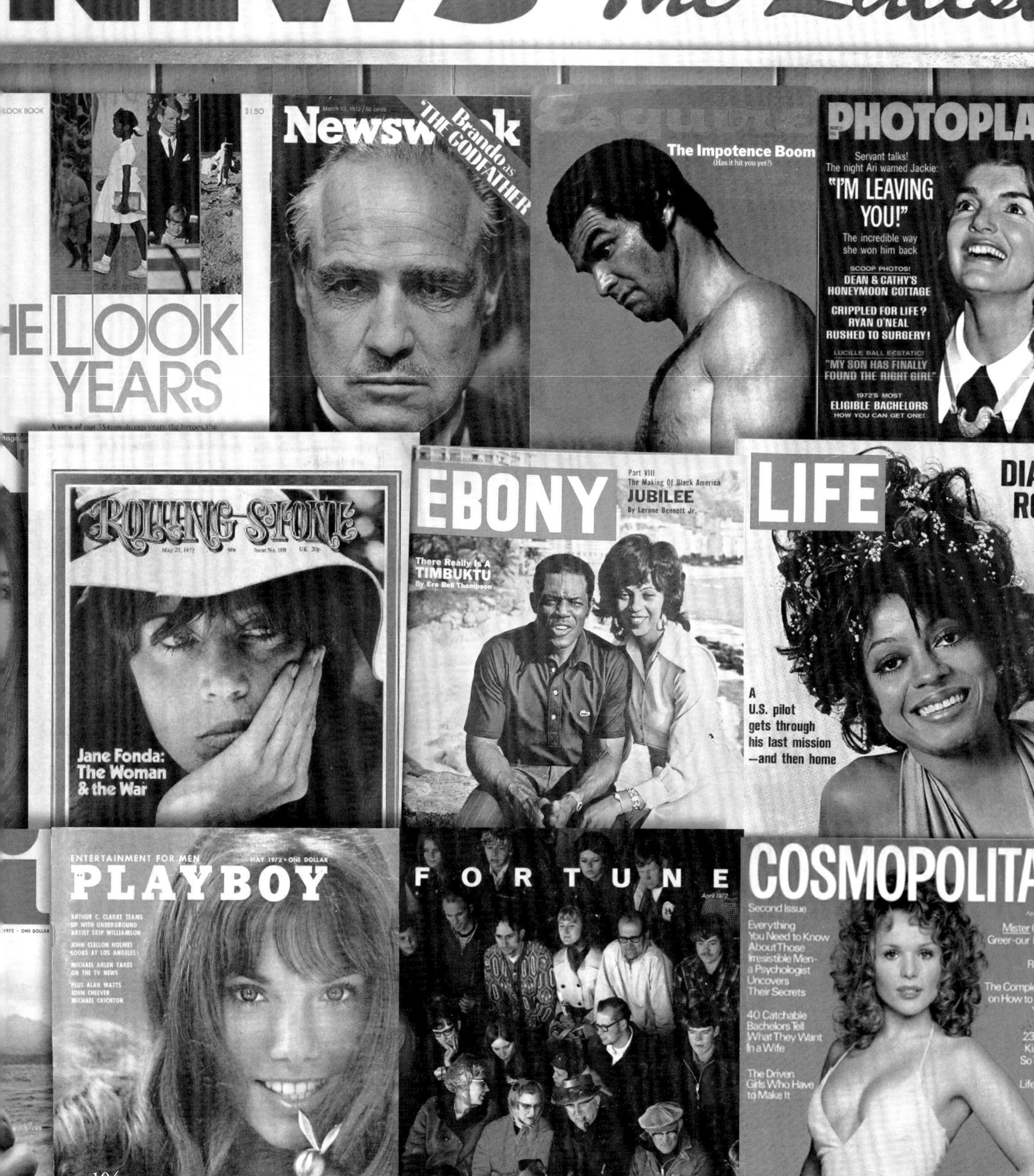

MAGAZINES

America's Only Rock 'n' Roll Magazine
December, 1972 15¢
CREEM
ussell:
ek in
urple
hrenia
wart
d Frothing

KATE MILLETT
ON THE TRIAL OF
ANGELA DAVIS
Ms.
WHAT
PAT NIXON WE
A FEMINIST JAN. 1
75¢
THE LIBERATED ORGASM — NEW FICTION BY DORIS LESSI
TEN YEARS LATER: THE REAL MARILYN MONROE
AUG(27)1972
THE WOMAN WHO DIED TOO SOON

VOGUE
how we
see you—
the
woman
of today
YOUR LOOK
the new easy chic for the woman
who asks a lot of her clothes
YOUR MAKEUP
a whole new look for day and night
YOUR HAIR
new length, new style...
new ways to care for it
BODY-TYPING
how to get the most out
of the body you've got
SUN-DRESSING
what you need wherever you go
ACUPUNCTURE
...why Western

Sports Illustrate
OCTOBER 16, 1972
PRO
BASKETBALL
IT ALL DEP
ON
LAKERS
13

FAMOUS
MONSTERS
OF FILMLAND
A WARREN MAGAZINE PDC 79¢
LOFF
ANEY JR.
ADINE
TRANGE
OL NAISH
US
BRAINS,
D
GOOEY
S!

MAD
No.154 Oct. '72
40¢

DC BATMAN
NO. 242
JUNE
30430
52
BIG pages
DON'T TAKE LESS
ONLY
25¢
BAT MAN
BRUCE
WAYNE
R.I.P.
COLLECTOR'S
SPECIAL!

Adventure
BIG BO
87
ALL
RIGHT, NUGGET...
STOP THAT
NONSENSE
AND
COME DOWN
AT ONCE!
STORIES · PUZZLES · FUN
...B
IT'S
CROW
...B
YO

ALL NEW STORIES
BEST IN COMICS
NOW
ONLY
20¢
DIANA PRINCE
WONDER WOMAN
NO. 201
AUG
30725
DIANA AND THE
AN LOCKED IN A
DUEL? AND
WHAT
IBA

DELL
1st COLLECTOR'S EDITION – SUPER LAUGH KIT!
CRACKED
SHUT-UP
SHUT-UPS · SHUT-UPS · SHUT

WHITMAN
BULLWINKLE
15¢
BULLWINKLE
and ROCKY

MARVEL COMICS G
MARVEL TEAM-UP
1
MAR
22147
20¢
MARVEL TEAM-U
FEATURING
SPIDER-MA
AND THE
HUMAN TORCH

RCA XL-100

It's more than just great color.

It's 100% Solid State AccuColor.®

XL-100 MODEL FQ-505 "COSMOS" (21" DIAGONAL). SIMULATED TV RECEPTION. CHASSIS SEGMENT REPOSITIONED FOR DEMONSTRATION.

XL-100 is color TV with circuitry designed to perform longer with fewer repairs.

There's not one chassis tube to burn out. We've replaced all tubes with 100% solid state components—the most reliable components used in television today. Twelve exclusive plug-in AccuCircuit modules control most set functions, so your service technician can make most repairs quickly and easily, in the home.

RCA's best color ever.

Every XL-100 console and table model has RCA's black matrix picture tube for the brightest, sharpest color in RCA history.

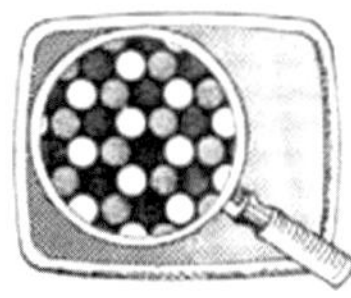

The tuning's a snap.

XL-100's advanced tuning system makes color tuning virtually foolproof! It features AccuMatic, RCA's color monitor that automatically locks color within a normal range.

Backed by the best warranty program ever.

We have such confidence in the reliability of XL-100, we back it for a *full year* on both parts and labor with our "Purchaser Satisfaction" warranty—"PS" for short. (See basic provisions below.)

Widest choice.

With over forty XL-100 models to choose from, there's an XL-100 that's right for your budget. Your RCA dealer can tell you more about why XL-100 is...

more than just great color.

PS Here are the basic provisions of our XL-100 "Purchaser Satisfaction" warranty ("PS" for short): If anything goes wrong with your new set within a year from the day you buy it, and it's our fault, we'll pay your repair bill—both parts and complete labor. You can use any service shop in which you have confidence— you don't have to pick from a special authorized list. If your set is a portable, you take it in for service. For larger sets, your serviceman will come to your home. Just present your warranty registration card and RCA pays his repair bill. If your picture tube becomes defective during the first two years we will exchange it for a rebuilt tube. (We pay for installation, during the first year—you pay for it in the second year.) In short, the warranty covers every set defect. It doesn't cover installation, foreign use, antenna systems or adjustment of customer controls.

Science

The Last Man on the Moon

December 7 - Apollo 17, the last manned Moon mission to date, launches with astronauts **Gene Cernan**, **Ronald Evans** and **Harrison Schmitt** aboard. The landing module touches down on the lunar surface at 2:55 pm EST on December 11, and Cernan becomes the last person to walk on the moon. Schmitt's reflection can just be made out in Cernan's helmet.

Space & Planetary Exploration

Apollo 17 astronauts take the famous "Blue Marble" photograph of the Earth.

Pioneer 10, the first man-made satellite to leave the solar system, is launched from Cape Kennedy.

The *Apollo 16* crew *(l-r)* **Ken Mattingly**, **John Young**, and **Charlie Duke**. They achieve a lunar rover speed record of 10.6 mph during their April, 1972 moon mission.

PHYSICS
**John Bardeen;
Leon Cooper;
John Robert
Schrieffer**
*BCS Theory of
Superconductors*

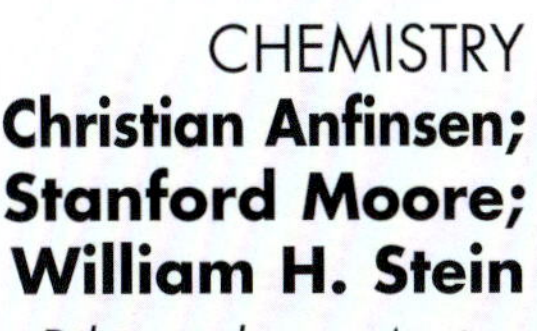

CHEMISTRY
**Christian Anfinsen;
Stanford Moore;
William H. Stein**
*Ribonuclease Amino
Acid Sequence*

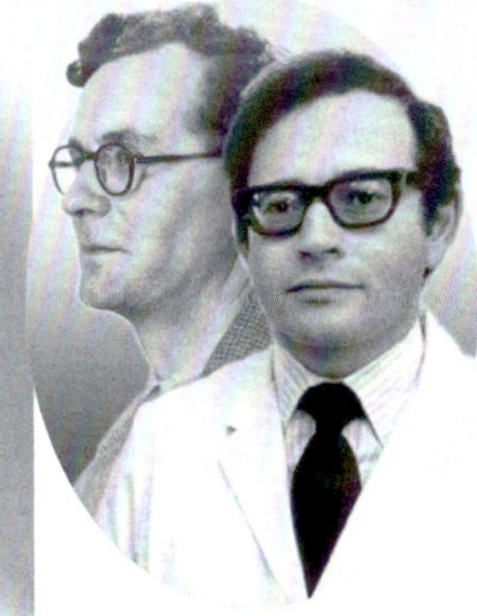

PHYSIOLOGY or
MEDICINE
**Gerald Edelman;
Rodney R. Porter**
*Immune System
Antibodies*

Dijkstra

THE TURING AWARD, named for British mathematician **Alan Turing**, is an annual prize given since 1966 to an individual selected for contributions "of lasting and major technical importance to the computer field." Dutch computer scientist **Edsger W. Dijkstra** receives the award in 1972 for his work in programming languages.

1972 had 4 eclipses — 2 solar eclipses and 2 lunar eclipses.

- January 16, 1972
Annular Solar Eclipse

- January 30, 1972
Total Lunar Eclipse

- July 10, 1972
Total Solar Eclipse

- July 25–26, 1972
Partial Lunar Eclipse

1972 MORTALITY RATES

- The incidence of fatal heart disease goes up 0.8%, from 358.4 per 100,000 persons in 1971 to 361.3 in 1972. The disease causes 741,010 deaths in 1971 and 752,450 in 1972.

- Cancer remains the second biggest killer, causing 166.6 deaths per 100,000.

- The death rate for motor vehicle accidents increas 6.7% over the previous year.

- Infant mortality rates are the lowest ever recorded.

1972 ADVERTISEMENT

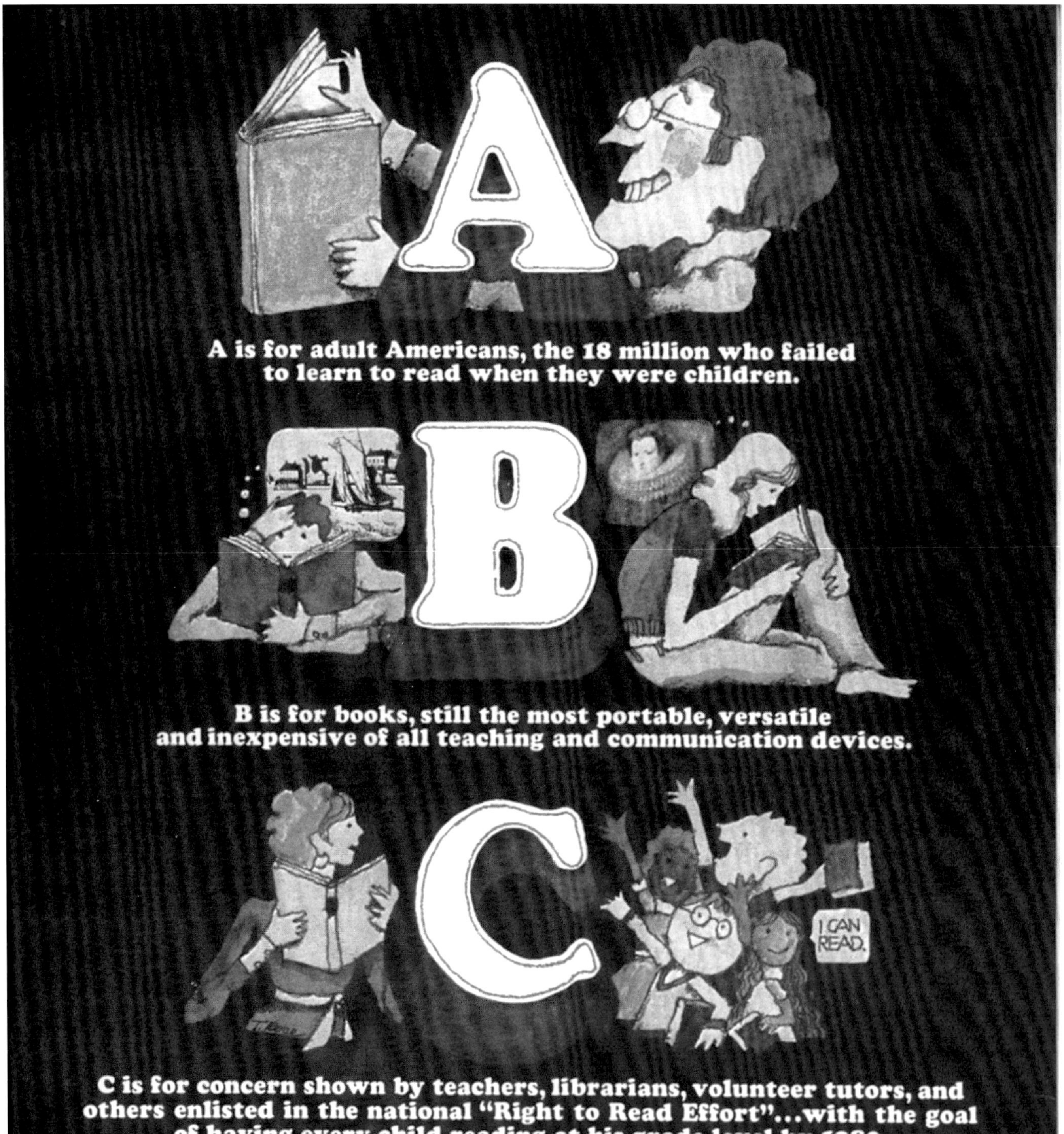

Rand McNally takes a very special interest in children learning their ABC's, and then learning to read books well enough to *enjoy* them. We are confident that the outstanding children's books and textbooks we publish and those we manufacture for other publishers are contributing to this end.

Rand McNally

publishers/book manufacturers/map makers

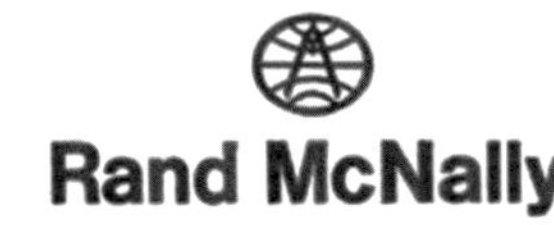

MEDICAL ADVANCES

Surgeons have developed effective replacements for arthritic knees and hips by the early 1970s, and joint replacement surgery becomes increasingly commonplace.

Computed Tomography (CT) imaging, or the "CAT Scan" is invented in 1972 by British engineer **Godfrey Hounsfield** and physicist **Allan Cormack** of Tufts University, Massachusetts, who are awarded the Nobel Peace Prize in 1979 for their contributions to medicine.

The first clinical CT scanners are installed between 1974 and 1976. Initially dedicated to head imaging only, whole body systems with larger patient openings became available in 1976. CT becomes widespread by the early '80s.

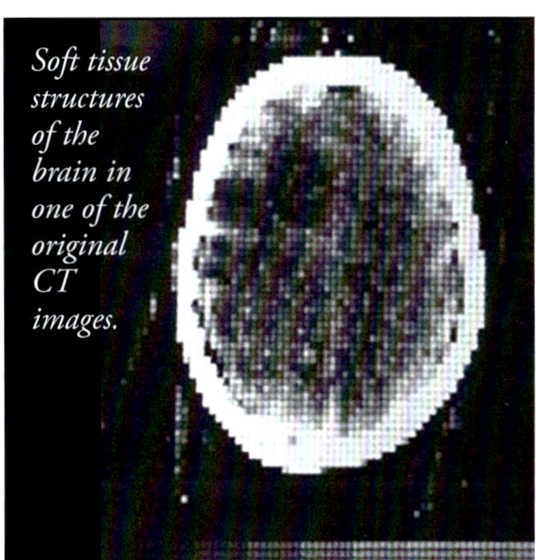
Soft tissue structures of the brain in one of the original CT images.

Meanwhile, Magnetic Resonance Imaging (MRI) is being developed and tested on multiple fronts during the 1970s, but most successfully by **John Mallard's** team at the University of Aberdeen. In 1980 they obtain the first clinically useful image of a patient's internal tissues, identifying tumours in the subject.

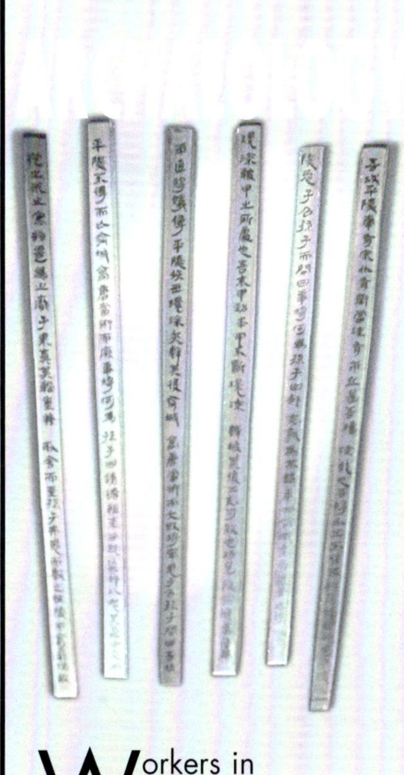

Workers in Shandong Province, China, accidentally unearth tombs at a construction site on April 10, 1972. Excavation of the Yinqueshan Han Tombs reveal a collection of thousands of 5th-century writings on bamboo slips including chapters from the fabled essay, *The Art of War*. *The Art of War* is an ancient military treatise dating from the 5th century BC attributed to the ancient Chinese military strategist, **Sun Tzu**.

THE BIG CAR INSIDE OUR LITTLE CAR.

Into each Vega a little Impala goes.

Power ventilation system.

Front disc brakes.

Side-guard door beams.

Two steel roofs instead of just one.

And, strange as it may seem, Vega's room-per-passenger compares pretty well with Impala's.

But Vega is no big car.

It's made for four people.

And although Vega's low center of gravity and wide stance make it feel bigger than a Vega, it's all done on a modest eight-foot wheelbase. (Two feet less than Impala's.)

Although our overhead-cam aluminum block engine is bigger than most little car engines, it's still awfully stingy with a gallon of gas.

And although Vega, with full foam seats and Full Coil suspension, is surprisingly comfortable to ride in from city to city, it's also a nifty car to zip around in from store to store.

Vega is a little car.

The little car that does everything well.

Chevrolet. Building a better way to see the U.S.A.

Highway safety begins at home. Buckle up before you leave.

BUSINESS

U.S. Federal Budget	**$229.2 B**
Inflation Rate	**3.21 %**
Unemployment	**5.8 %**

1972
Average Movie Ticket Price: $1.70
Inflation Adjusted: $10.13

Top-Grosser of the Year: The Godfather

1972
The Cost of a First-Class Stamp Holds Steady at 8¢
Inflation Adjusted: $.51

1972 Price of **ONE GALLON of GAS**

36¢
Inflation Adjusted: $2.28

Federal Minimum Wage: $1.60 an hour for non-farm workers.

Median Annual U.S. Family Income: $11,120
The median family income for black families in the U.S. is $6,860 — about 59% of the income of white families. The income for women is about 57% of the income of men.

Average Annual U.S. Earnings for:

Professional	$17,052
Farmers	$8,303
Farm Labor	$5,970
Managers/Admin.	$16,901
Clerical	$11,412
Sales	$14,292
Craftsmen	$12,713
Housekeepers	$3,121
Service Workers	$9,386
Laborers	$9,421
Teacher	$10,174

"Adjusted for inflation, average weekly earnings for production and nonsupervisory employees — the bulk of the workforce — topped out in October 1972."
- *The Wall Street Journal*
April 17, 2015

THE FEDERAL BUDGET DOLLAR
Fiscal Year 1972 Estimate

Where it comes from...

Where it goes...

Average Cost of a New House in 1972

$27,592.⁰⁰

Median House Prices

Boston	$24,700
Chicago	$19,900
Cleveland	$28,900
Denver	$19,700
Houston	$22,000
Los Angeles	$19,100
New York	$18,600

Average Monthly Rent: $155.⁰⁰

Least-Expensive '72 Cars

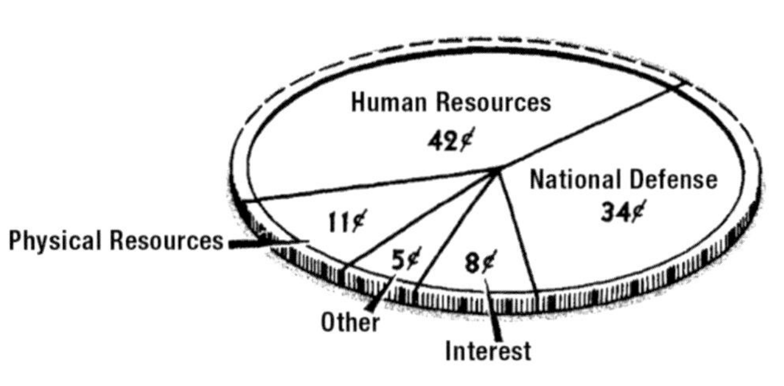

Ford Pinto 2-door	$1,931	base
+ Automatic transmission	$170	
+ AM radio	$60	
	$2,161	
AMC Gremlin 2-door sedan	$1,999	base
+ Automatic transmission	$200	
+ AM radio	$66	
	$2,265	
Chevrolet Vega 2-door	$2,031	base
+ Automatic transmission	$193	
+ AM radio	$59	
	$2,283	

Most-Expensive '72 Cars

Lincoln Continental Mark IV	$8,605	base
+ Power sunroof	$611	
	$9,216	
Cadillac Fleetwood Brougham	$7,569	base
+ Power sunroof	$610	
	$8,179	
Cadillac Fleetwood Eldorado Convertible	$7,495	base
+ Automatic climate control	$523	
	$8,018	

1972 Dow Jones Industrial Average
Average Closing Price: 950.08 Year High: 1,036.27

The Dow in the 1970s

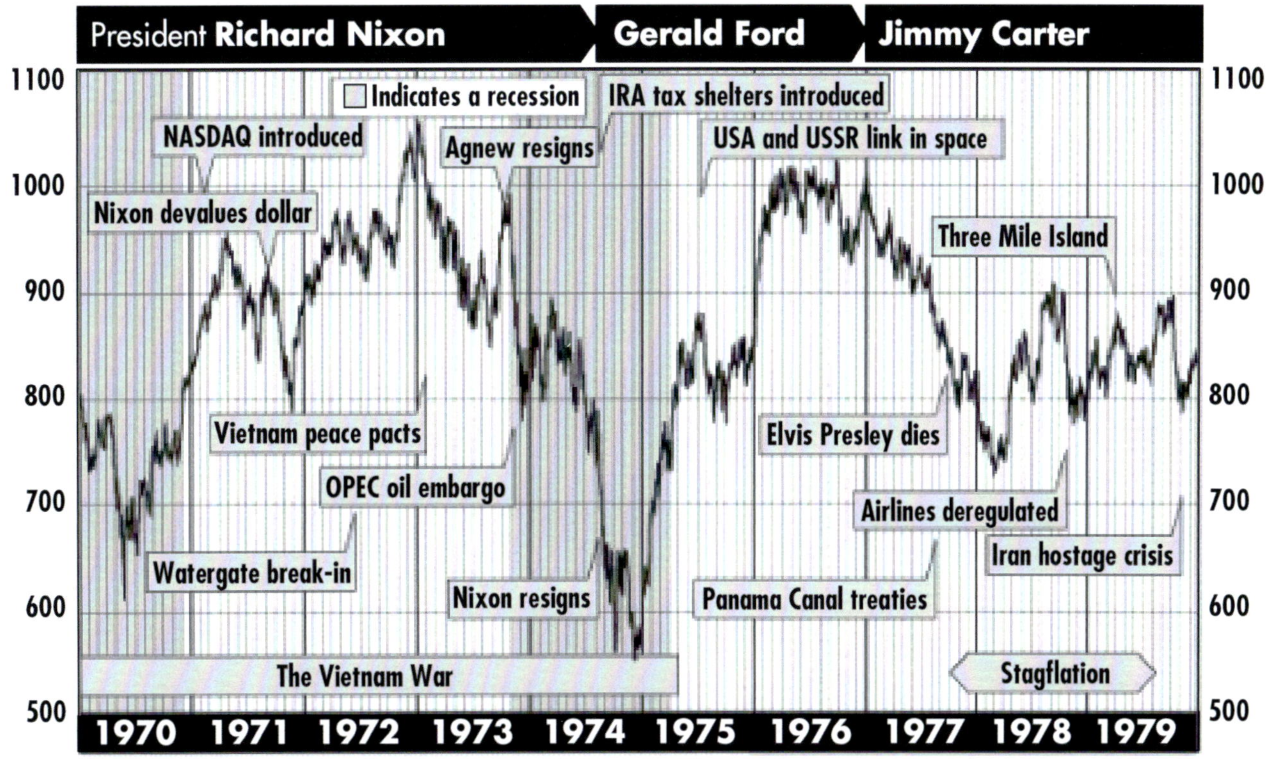

On November 14, 1972, with a growing economy and surging corporate profits, the Dow Jones Industrial Average (DJIA) crosses the 1,000-point mark for the first time, with a total volume of 20.2 million shares traded.

• TOP 10 RANKED BUSINESSES IN THE DOW •

	Company	Revenues ($ millions)	Profits ($ millions)
1	**General Motors**	28,263.9	1,935.7
2	**Exxon Mobil**	18,700.6	1,461.6
3	**Ford Motor**	16,433.0	656.7
4	**General Electric**	9,425.3	471.8
5	**Intl. Business Machines (IBM)**	8,273.6	1,078.8
6	**Mobil**	8,243.0	540.8
7	**Chrysler**	7,999.3	83.7
8	**Texaco**	7,529.1	903.9
9	**ITT Industries**	7,345.8	336.8
10	**AT&T Technologies**	6,045.2	258.4

The U.S. Census Bureau provides data on minority-owned and women-owned businesses for the first time in 1972.

ALICE COOPER
COOPER KILLER / ALICE COOPER

AQUALUNG
JETHRO TULL
ALBUMS

Reg. 4.47   **3.96**

Reg. 3.47   **2.96**

Excellent Selection To Choose From

great buys
FOR A MAN'S SUMMER

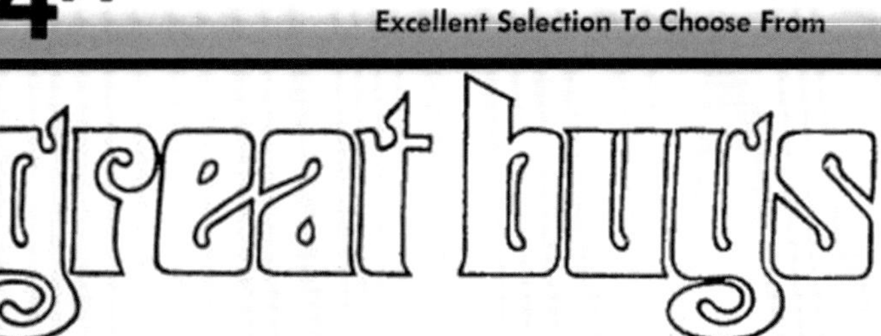

SUITS
By Michael
Stern-Cricketeer - J&J
Wool and Dacron — Double Knits

$75.00 UP

SPORT COATS

$55.00 UP

SHIRTS
By Van Heusen
Holbrook - Dress and Sports

$6.00 UP

SLACKS
By Mayfair, Mayer
Cricketeer — Largest Selection Ever

$15.00 UP

HATS
By Dobbs

SHOES
By Portage - Solids - T...

THE PRICE
THAT WAS

13 MORE DAYS AT CURRENT PRICES!

The Ardmore
$23,700

Price Includes: Kiln Dried Lumber, Porches, Dishwasher, Insulated Windows, Brick Front and Full Tiled Bathrooms.

Possessing a stately appearance, this BiLevel Titan colonial creates just the mood for those with discriminating taste. Its mid-level entry creates added character to first and second levels. This is a lot of house for the investment because of its compact design. It features four bedrooms, 2 baths, plus a nice size family room.

Titan Homes
for today's living.

NEW '72 TORINO 2 DR. HARDTOP
Includes all standard factory equipment.
$2449

ALL PRICES INCLUDE FREIGHT AND DEALER PREPARATION!

NEW 1972 FORD PICKUP
$2349
Includes All Standard Factory Equipment.

NEW 1972 PINTO
$1949
Includes All Standard Factory Equipment.

NEW 1972 MAVERICK
$2149
Includes All Standard Factory Equipment.

Vicky Vaughn Layers in Plaid.

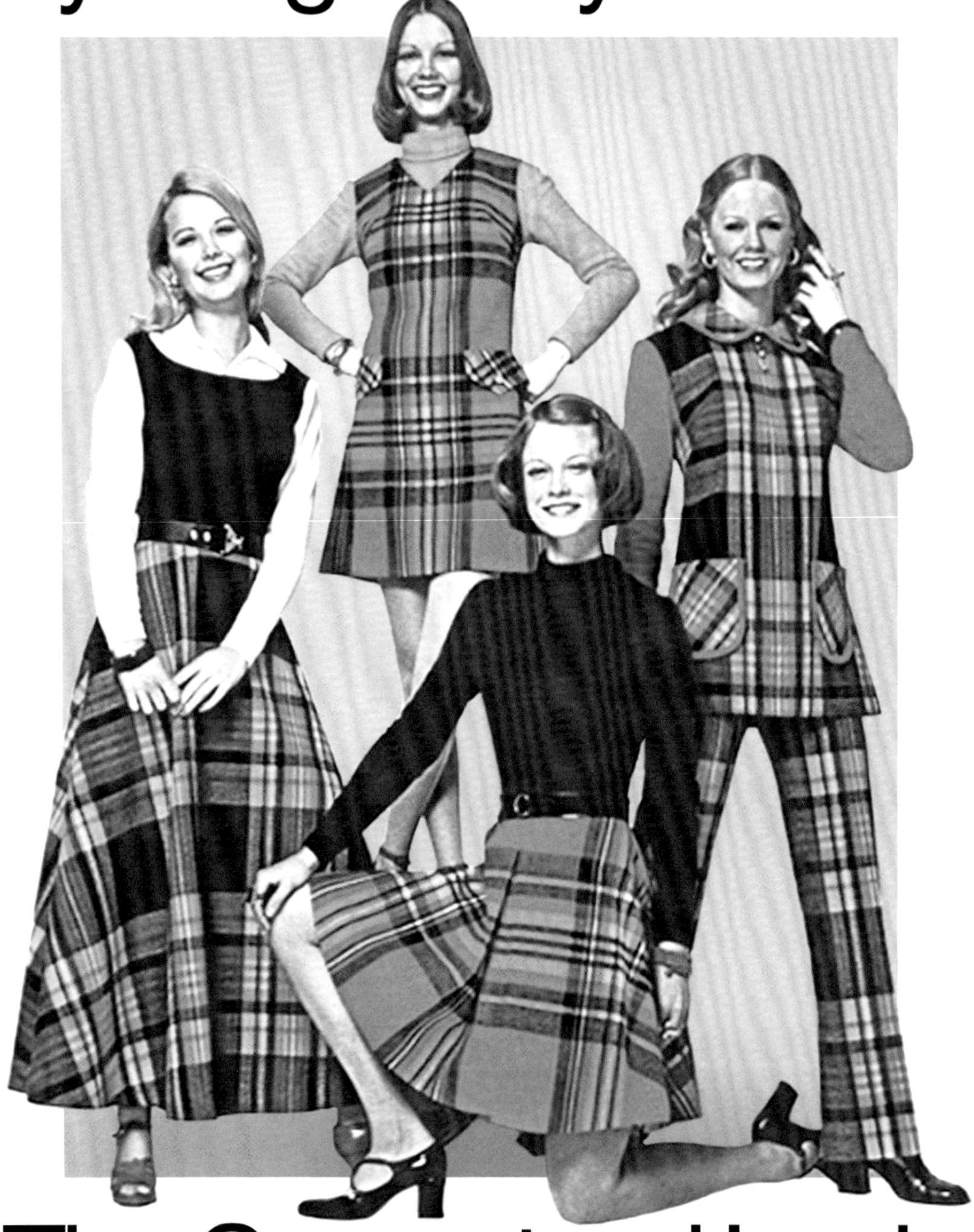

The Guaranteed Look.

Plaids 'n Lassies. Lively layered looks in woven Acrilan® acrylic with rib-knit combos. The all day long, about 32.00 Jumper plus turtle shell, about 28.00. The sweatered whirl, about 26.00. Pantsuit pow, about 32.00. Red or black predominate in plaids. 5-15. Wear Dated® and guaranteed for one full year's normal wear, refund or replacement when returned with tag and sales slip to Monsanto. Prices slightly higher in the West. At these atores and their branches and many others: Auerbach Co., Salt Lake City; L.S. Ayres & Co., Indianapolis; Bloomingdale's, New York; Filene's, Boston; The J.L. Hudson Co., Detroit; Marshall Field & Co., Chicago; Roos-Atkins, San Francisco; Tilche-Goettinger Co., Dallas. Or write R. and M. Kaufmann, 1400 Broadway, New York 10018. In New Zealand, Maida Vale, Ltd. In Mexico, Sherel, S.A.

You get what you pay for or we pay for it.

1972 fashion
PLAIDS
PRINTS
STRIPES
TWEEDS
are all in the fashion playbook
&
CHEMISTRY BRINGS US FABULOUS, FLUID, STRETCH FABRICS
DENIMS absolutely still in!

FASHION

HALSTON

Considered by many fashionistas as the best designer of easy and fancy ready-wear, Halston earns the **"Winnie"** (Women's Wear Award) at the Coty American Fashion Critics' Awards.

Halston designs for New York night-life. One of his most iconic designs, the silk jersey halter dress is a staple among the rich, famous and the fashionable. The halter look is repackaged for Vogue Pattern (left) featuring Qiana — synthetic nylon jersey — by Jerry Silverman.

Halston introduces Ultrasuede material to popular culture, as seen in a shirt-dress (left). No doubt his line was influenced by **Vera Maxwell** (shirt-dress, see right) who took a significant risk in 1971 to purchase 30,000 yards of a new fabric called Ultrasuede produced by a company in Japan. Initially buyers were afraid to purchase clothes made of the new material, but time proved Maxwell right and the fabric became identified with her designs.

NOTABLES

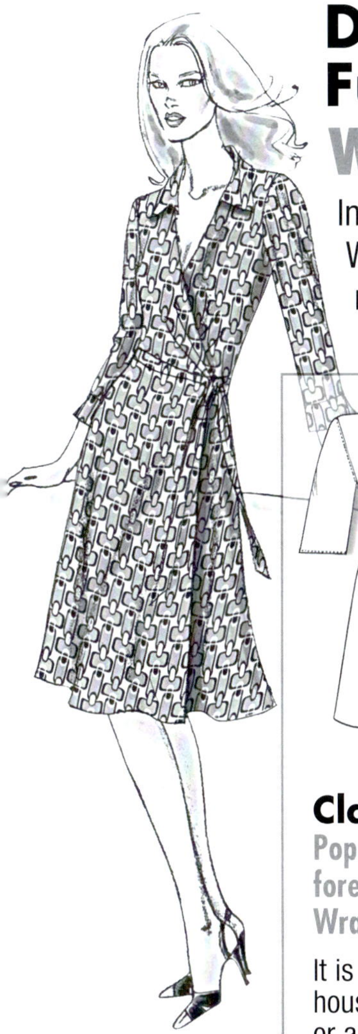

Diane von Furstenberg WRAP DRESS

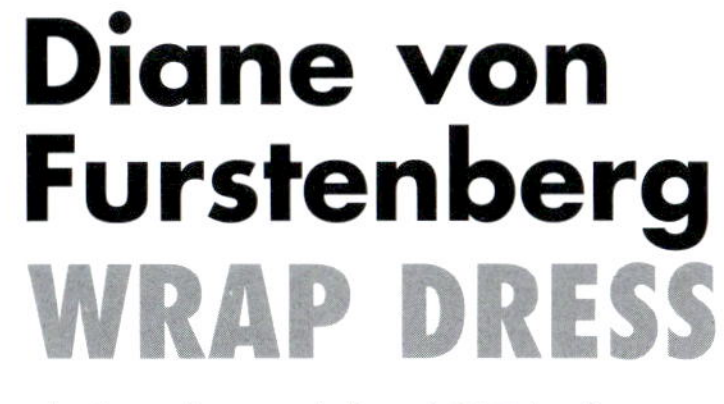

Introduced in 1971, her Wrap Dress becomes a retail success in 1972 for her label.

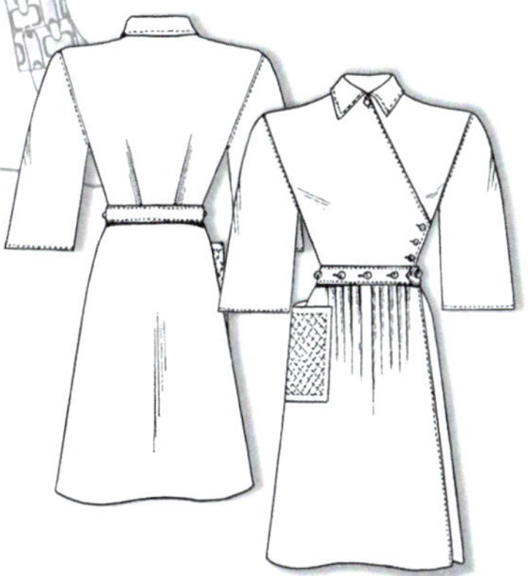

Claire McCardell's Popover Dress of 1942 foreshadowed Furstenberg's Wrap Dress.

It is designed to be worn as a housedress, a dressing gown or a party dress.

BETSEY JOHNSON OF ALLEY CAT®

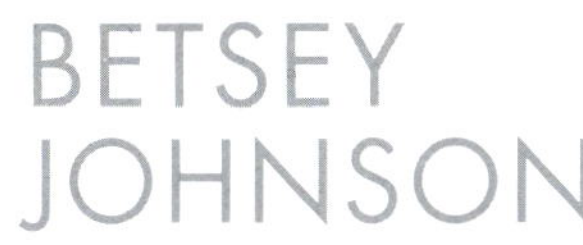

Last year's winner of the Coty Fashion Critics' "Winnie" Award, still turning heads with her youthful, colorful outlandish designs.

COTY American Fashion Critics Hall of Fame

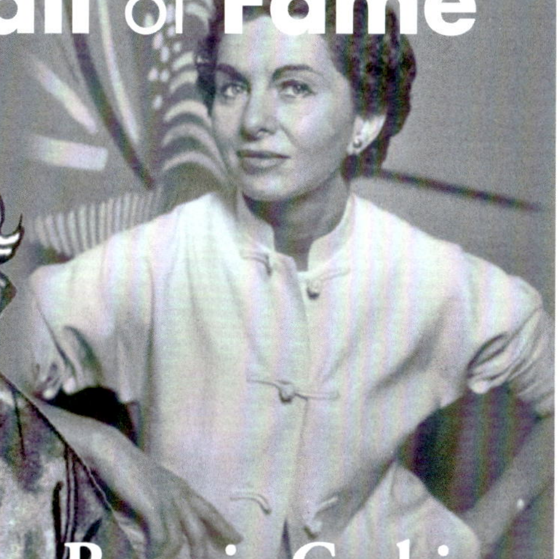

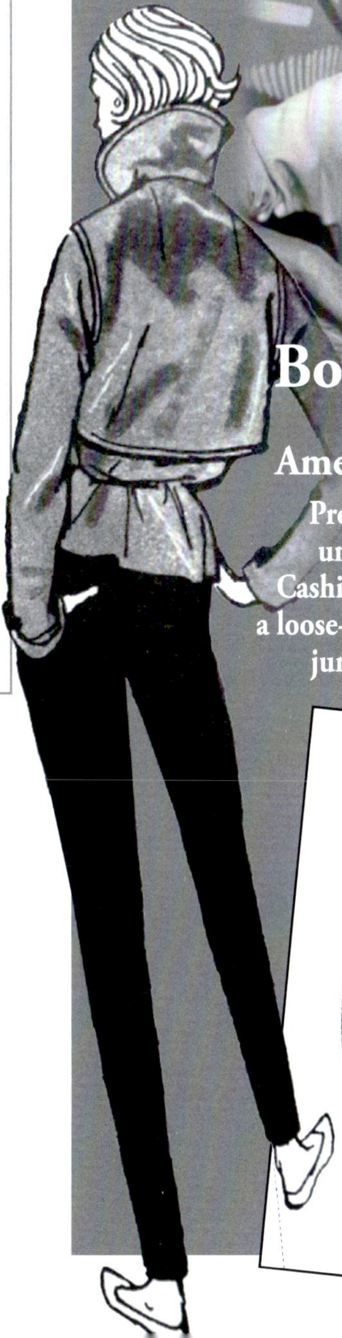

Bonnie Cashin

"Mother of American Sportswear"

Proponent of functional, uncomplicated designs, Cashin's contribution includes a loose-fitting, slip-on turtleneck, jumpsuits, and ponchos.

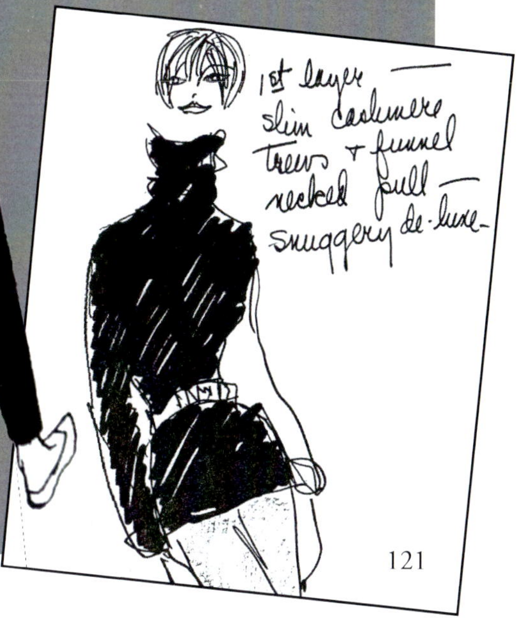

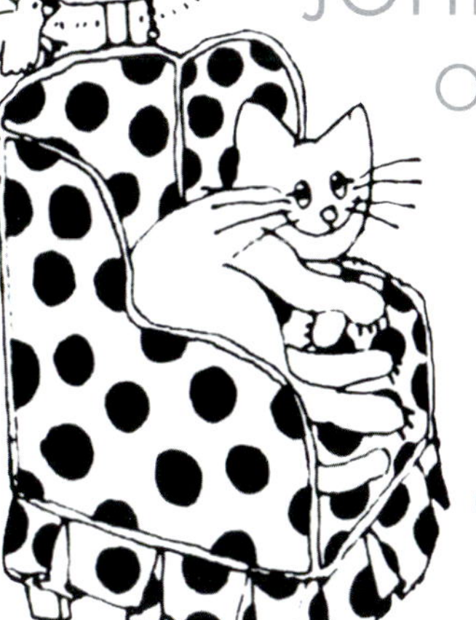

SURE, COME AS YOU ARE...

The Sixties' CounterCulture dress codes become the norm for the Seventies.

1972 welcomes personal fashion expressions. The new lax dress codes are seen in some corporate settings, like advertising agencies – blue jeans, dashikis & beachwear are welcome. Suits are optional — don't forget your surfboard!

Shane Gould
Australian Freestyle Swimming Champion: 5 individual medals: 3 gold, 1 silver & 1 bronze.

OLYMPIC SWIM EVENTS
21 of 22 RECORDS BROKEN
SYNTHETIC FABRIC, SPANDEX, LYCRA & ELASTANE,
with exceptional elasticity and lightness, reduces water drag — a game-changer for swimmers!

White Stag-Speedo selected for the 1972 Olympic Swimmers and Water Polo Team.

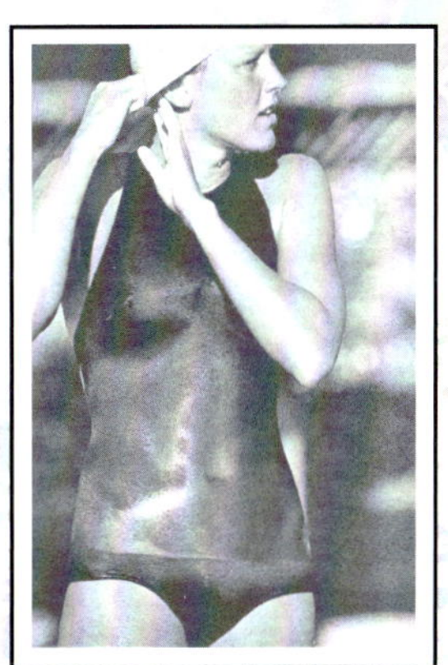

The pioneer skinsuit worn by the East Germans at the 1972 Games is made of a very fine rubberized cotton that, when wet, is virtually transparent.

BASEBALL
abandons **BELTS** **& BUTTONS!**

Oakland A's REGGIE JACKSON, SAL BANDO, MIKE EPSTEIN & JOE RUDI.

The San Francisco Giants chuck the old flannels for pullover jerseys and beltless pants.

Juan Marichal claims that "double-knits will stretch and make it easier when I kick high. That's very important."
-- *Sporting News*

THE LOOK OF EASE: BELTLESS PANTS

Dusty Baker of the Atlanta Braves debuts new uniform.

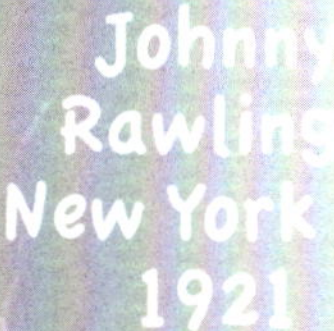

GREY FLANNEL suits any man
GREY FLANNEL
Cologne
GEOFFREY BEENE
NEW YORK
BEENE
AT MACY'S

"In the Heat of Summer, 'Ice Cream Suit' Makes a Comeback"

August 1972, New York Times

Permanent press, machine-washable light-weight jackets and trousers of polyester and cotten blend brings men's wear back to the carefree Ivy League styles, made fashionable by Brooks Brothers. Mostly, this look brings to mind Mark Twain and the southern ease.

"Twain's Fancy Suit"
He unveiled his signature style on December 7, 1906, at age 71.

Mark Twain with one of his rented cats, Sackcloth or Ashes.

Photography by Frances Benjamin Johnson

Brooks English
white calfskin
oxford.

Left:
Easy wear & Easy care
by Haspel Bros.
...very much like this year's
Striped Suit by Pierre Cardin

Spend the winter in lush angora without spending the winter paying for it.

If you want to bundle up in soft, warm angora this season but you don't want to spend a bundle, come to Ohrbach's. Take your pick of a dress or a pants outfit for just **$65.**

We have an angora and lamb's-wool sweater dress that will take you beautifully from the afternoon into the evening. It's grown-up and elegant in baby soft colors of pink, blue, and yellow.

We combined a sweater of angora and lamb's-wool with knit palazzo pants to come up with an outfit that's both comfortable and luxurious. The dolman-sleeve sweater comes in pastel shades of heather beige and light blue. The pants are dyed to match.

So remember: angora weather is just around the corner and prices are at record lows at Ohrbach's.

It's what you get for the low price that counts. Ohrbach's.

FAMOUS BIRTHS

Gwyneth Paltrow

Sept. 27 / Actress, influencer

From *Vanity Fair's* *Best Dressed List*

Marisa Berenson Yves Saint Laurent dubbed her "the girl of the Seventies"

Jane Engelhard International Best Dressed List Hall of Fame. (Vanity Fair)

Harry Belafonte "King of Calypso" American singer, songwriter, activist and actor

PASSINGS

Cristóbal Balenciaga

(January 21, 1895, Getaria, Spain – March 23, 1972, Xàbia, Spain)

Spanish Basque fashion designer, trained as a tailor, and the founder of the Balenciaga fashion house. He had a reputation as a couturier of uncompromising standards. He was hailed as "the master of us all" by Christian Dior.

> **66** ...the only couturier in the truest sense of the word.
>
> • • •
>
> The others are simply fashion designers. **99**
>
> *Coco Chanel*

Balenciaga made cocoon coats, balloon skirts, high-low hems, tunic dresses, chemise dresses and empire waistlines famous. He rose to prominence after World War II and established his own brand. His most famous clients were Mona von Bismarck, Grace Kelly, Ava Gardner, Audrey Hepburn and Jackie Kennedy. He defiantly resisted the rules, guidelines, and bourgeoisie status of the Chambre Syndicale de la Haute Couture Parisienne. Although he is revered, technically, Balenciaga couture was never haute couture — and apparently, he was proud of it.

Cristóbal Balenciaga closed his fashion house in 1968.

Norman Norell

Norman David Levinson (April 20, 1900 – October 25, 1972) American fashion designer whose influence spanned from the Ziegfeld Follies to couture houses, thus earning the moniker, "The American Balenciaga." Marilyn Monroe, a big fan of Norell, famously wore his unforgettable deep-V sequin dress to the 1962 Golden Globes and a peasant neckline dress on her wedding day (to Arthur Miller, 1956).

Norell was the first recipient of the American Fashion Critics Award in 1943 (later called the Coty Fashion Award). His second Coty Award came in 1951 and the Critics' Hall of Fame award in 1956.

Marilyn Monroe

When Cliff Richey takes off his Purcells, he puts on his Purcells.

Cliff Richey wears Purcells off the court. And on.

So before he takes on the toughest pros in tennis, he takes off his leather Purcell RaceArounds.

Then he puts on his on-the-court, rugged Purcells. The ones he wears in championship tennis matches.

The ones with the tough, durable insole.

(Cliff has never had a Purcell insole breakdown, and he often skids to a stop and can burn out the bottom of a shoe in five days.)

A good insole, to Cliff is what comfort's all about. Ours is the best he's found. In fact, he says this shoe is so comfortable, you forget you have it on.

Which is a good way for you to remember Purcells.

Wherever you buy better shoes.

Jack Purcell

B.F.Goodrich
...in pursuit of excellence

SPORTS

THE OLYMPIC YEAR

The Games of the XX Olympiad, taking place August 26 to September 11, 1972, are the second Summer Olympics to be held in Germany. The country is hopeful that a successful Munich Summer Olympics will expunge the shadow cast by the 1936 Berlin Games, which infamously took place under the Nazis. Even the 1972 Game's motto, *"The Cheerful Games,"* proclaims positivity. Unfortunately, much of that optimism is dashed in the second week by the Munich massacre, in which eleven Israeli athletes and coaches and a West German police officer are killed by Palestinian Black September terrorists.

SUMMER STARS

American swimmer **Mark Spitz** sets a world record by winning seven gold medals in a single Olympics — an achievement that will stand for 36 years. Spitz previously won two golds and a bronze in the Mexico City games.

Soviet gymnast **Olga Korbut** earns 3 golds & a silver and captures hearts on the balance beam and floor & team exercises. She also takes another silver & gold in 1976.

The 3 Seconds

The Olympic Men's Basketball Final takes a controversial turn when, with no time remaining, the U.S. team posts an apparent 50-49 victory over the Soviet Union. Scorers then reset the clock to add a questionable 3 seconds to the end of the game after time had officially expired. The Soviets are allowed 3 more attempts until they finally score, winning the game, 51-50. In protest, the U.S. players skip the medal ceremony, refusing their second-place medals. The silver medals still sit in a vault in Lausanne, Switzerland.

SUMMEROLYMPICSSUMMEROLYMPICSSUMMEROLYMPICS

Munich 1972

THE FIRST OFFICIAL SUMMER OLYMPIC MASCOT!

15-year-old Australian swimmer **Shane Gould** wins three gold medals, setting a world record in each race, as well as a silver and a bronze.

"Waldi" is a long-haired breed of Dachshund popular in Bavaria for it's tenacity & agility.

Poster art by David Hockney

Olympische Spiele München 1972

"Sugar" **Ray Seales** is the only American Boxer to win a gold medal (light welterweight) in the '72 Summer Olympics.

OHH NOOO...!

U.S. world record holders **Eddie Hart** and **Rey Robinson** miss their quarterfinal sprints, having been given the wrong starting time. They watch live TV coverage of the races they should have been in.

MEDAL TABLE			
NATION	GOLD	SILVER	BRONZE
Soviet Union	50	27	22
United States	33	31	30
East Germany	20	23	23
West Germany	13	11	16
Japan	13	8	8
Australia	8	7	2
Poland	7	5	9
Hungary	6	13	16
Bulgaria	6	10	5
Italy	5	3	10
Sweden	4	6	6
Great Britain	4	5	9
Romania	3	6	7
Cuba	3	1	4
Finland	3	1	4
Netherlands	3	1	1
France	2	4	7
Czechoslovakia	2	4	2
Kenya	2	3	4
Yugoslavia	2	1	2
Norway	2	1	1
North Korea	1	1	3
New Zealand	1	1	1
Uganda	1	1	0
Denmark	1	0	0

MEDAL TABLE			
NATION	GOLD	SILVER	BRONZE
Switzerland	0	3	0
Canada	0	2	3
Iran	0	2	1
Belgium	0	2	0
Greece	0	2	0
Austria	0	1	2
Colombia	0	1	2
Argentina	0	1	0
Lebanon	0	1	0
Mexico	0	1	0
Mongolia	0	1	0
Pakistan	0	1	0
South Korea	0	1	0
Tunisia	0	1	0
Turkey	0	1	0
Brazil	0	0	2
Ethiopia	0	0	2
Ghana	0	0	1
India	0	0	1
Jamaica	0	0	1
Niger	0	0	1
Nigeria	0	0	1
Spain	0	0	1

WINTEROLYMPICSWINTEROLYMPICSWINTEROLYMPICS

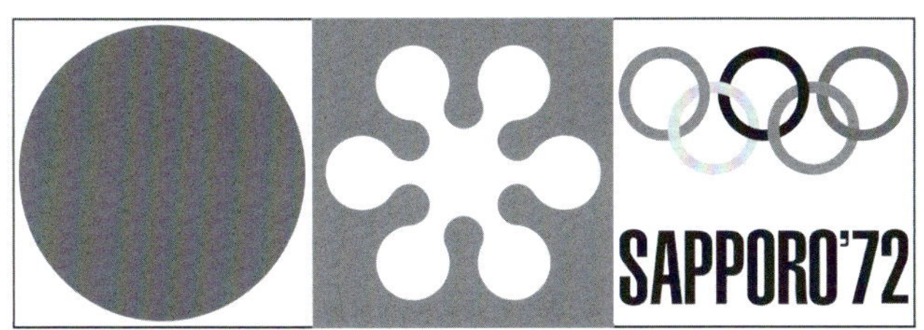

札幌オリンピック

February 3 - February 13
Sapporo, Hokkaido, Japan

The first Winter Olympic Games to take place outside Europe and North America.

EXTRAVAGANT MEMORABLE EVENT

The Japanese government spends a great deal of money to create a memorable Olympics – the Games are the most extravagant to date. To defray the high expenses, the organizers sell the television rights for over $8 million.

THE FIRST EVER GOLD MEDAL for Japan in the Winter Olympics

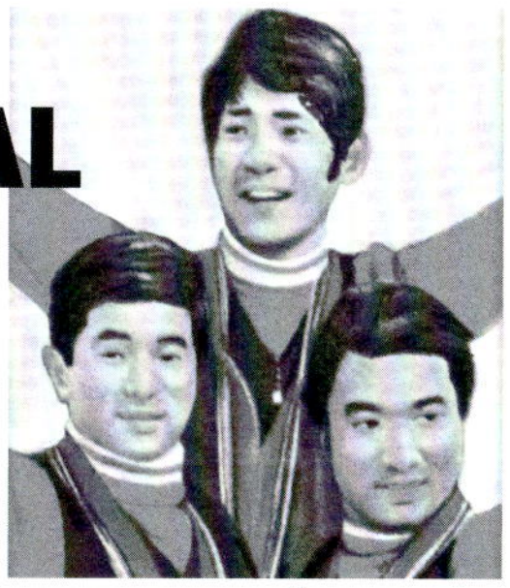

Three Japanese athletes win big in ski jump events. **Yukio Kasaya** takes the gold, **Akisugo Konno** earns silver and **Seiji Aochi** wins bronze.

MEDAL TABLE

NATION	GOLD	SILVER	BRONZE
Soviet Union	8	5	3
East Germany	4	3	7
Switzerland	4	3	3
Netherlands	4	3	2
United States	3	2	3
West Germany	3	1	1
Norway	2	5	5
Italy	2	2	1
Austria	1	2	2
Sweden	1	1	2
Japan	1	1	1
Czechoslovakia	1	0	2
Poland	1	0	0
Spain	1	0	0
Finland	0	4	1
France	0	1	2
Canada	0	1	0

FIRST GOLD FOR SPAIN IN THE WINTER OLYMPICS

"Paquito" Fernandez Ochoa wins the slalom by a full second.

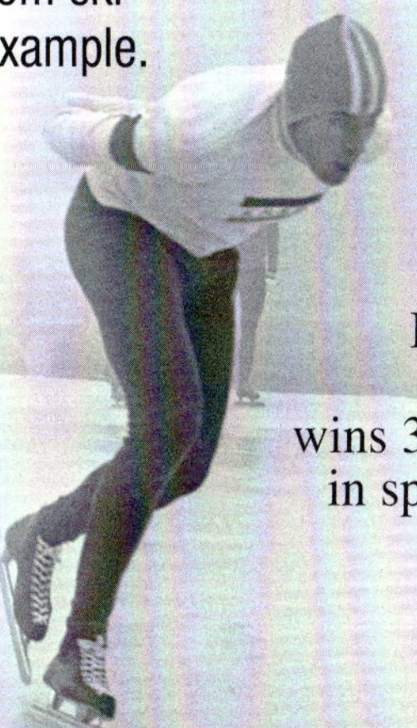

The Sapporo Winter Olympics introduces an adorable bear called **TAKUCHAN** as the unofficial mascot.

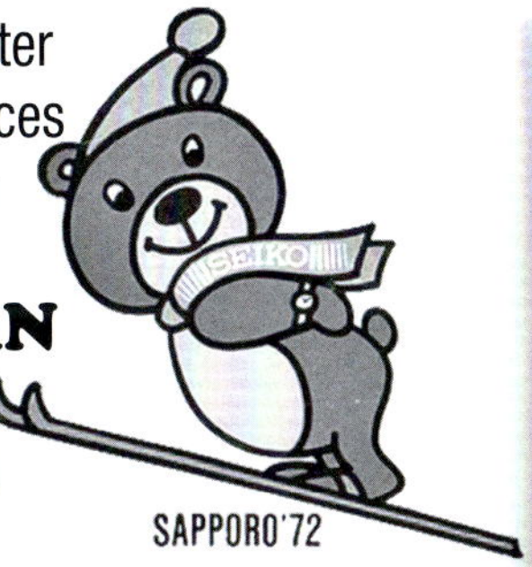

THREE DAYS BEFORE THE GAMES, a controversy arises over amateur status. IOC president **Avery Brundage** threatens to disqualify 40 Alpine skiers who receive endorsement deals. Austrian skier **Karl Schranz**, who received over $50,000 per year from ski manufacturers, is banned as an example.

MEANWHILE... Canada refuses to send an ice hockey team, asserting that professional ice hockey players from Communist nations are allowed to compete with no restrictions.

American skater **JANET LYNN**, a bronze medal winner, is overwhelmingly popular with the Japanese media.

Dutch skater **Ard Schenk**, wins 3 gold medal in speed skating.

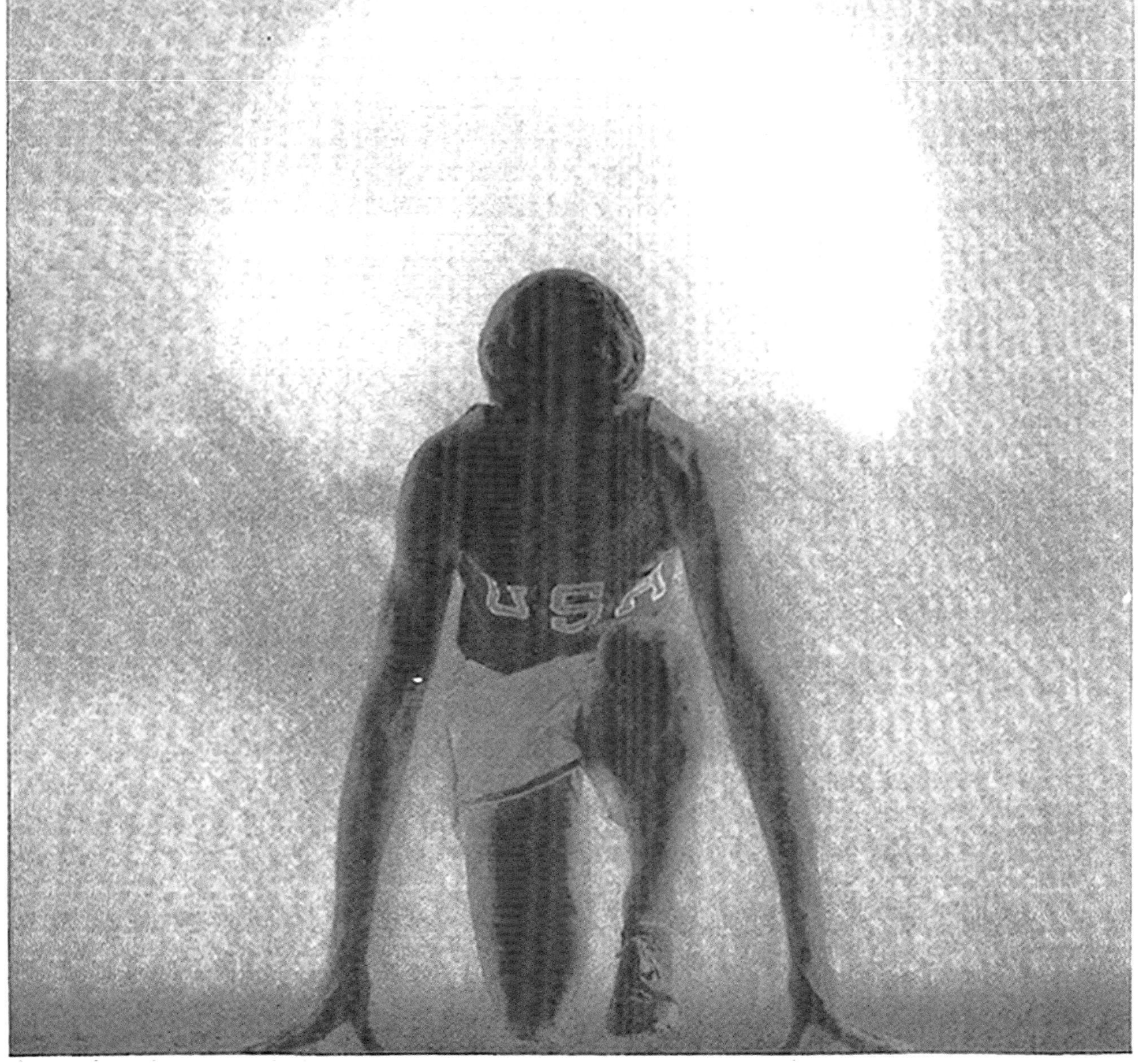
ABC Sports brings you the greatest athletes under the sun.
Starting August 25, ABC Sports will bring you an unprecedented two weeks of total prime time coverage of the 1972 Summer Olympics from Munich, Germany.
ABC Television Network
USA

MOST VALUABLE PLAYER

NATIONAL LEAGUE
Johnny Bench (Cincinnati Reds)

AMERICAN LEAGUE
Dick Allen (Chicago White Sox)

HOME RUN LEADERS

NATIONAL LEAGUE
Johnny Bench (Cincinnati Reds, 40)

AMERICAN LEAGUE
Dick Allen (Chicago White Sox, 37)

BATTING CHAMPIONS

NATIONAL LEAGUE
Billy Williams (Chicago Cubs, .333)

AMERICAN LEAGUE
Rod Carew (Minnesota Twins, .318)

ROOKIE OF THE YEAR

NATIONAL LEAGUE
Jon Matlack (New York Mets)

AMERICAN LEAGUE
Carlton Fisk (Boston Red Sox)

MAJOR LEAGUE ALL-STAR GAME
ATLANTA STADIUM

On July 25, the **American League** and the **National League** faced off (most players, in their team's new double knit uniforms). The National League walks away with a 4-3 wins in 10 innings. Sadly, this was the final All-Star Game for **Roberto Clemente** before his death in a New Year's Eve plane crash.

THE MUSTACHE GANG

(left to right) Bob Locker, Mike Epstein, Reggie Jackson, Darrell Knowles and Rollie Fingers

Baseball
1972 World Series

OAKLAND ATHLETICS *over* CINCINNATI REDS 4-3

The Oakland Athletics, without their injured star right fielder, **Reggie Jackson**, wins the first two games of the World Series in Cincinnati and go on to win their first World Series since 1930. A's catcher/first baseman **Gene Tenace** leads the way with four home runs and nine RBIs, winning the MVP award.

- 1972 BASEBALL -
Hall of Fame Inductees

Election to the Hall of Fame follows the system established in 1971. The Baseball Writers' Association of America selects 3 MLB players. The Veterans Committee selects 3. The Negro Leagues Committee selects 2 players.

Yogi Berra
Catcher / Coach / Manager
NY Mets, NY Yankees, Houston Astros

Sandy Koufax
Pitcher: Brooklyn Dodgers, Los Angeles Dodgers

Vernon Louis "Lefty" Gomez
Pitcher: New York Yankees, Washington Senators

William "Will" Harridge
American League President

Ross Youngs
Right Fielder: NY Giants

Joshua "Josh" Gibson
Catcher: (NL) Homestead Grays, Pittsburgh Crawfords; (Other L) Dragones de Ciudad Trujillo, Azules de Veracruz
Gibson never played in the major leagues due to the unwritten agreement that prevented non-white players from participating.

Walter Fenner "Buck" Leonard
First Baseman: (NL) Homestead Grays; Algodoneros de Torreón, Minor Leagues, Durango

Sandy Koufax, youngest member ever elected.

Early "Gus" Wynn Jr.
Pitcher: Washington Senators, Cleveland Indians, Chicago White Sox

FOOT

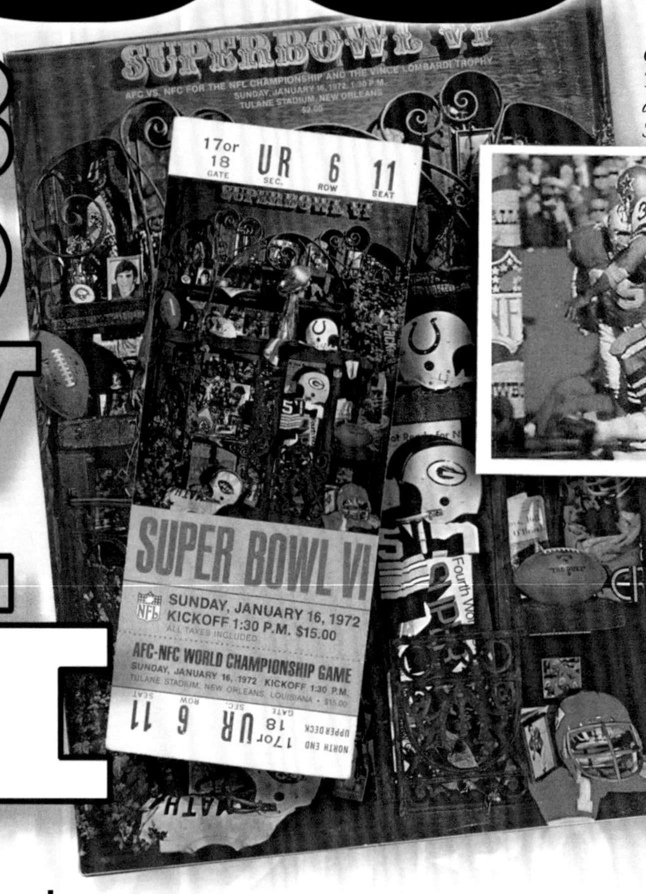

Cowboys running back **Duane Thomas** rushes for a touchdown against the Dolphins in Super Bowl VI.

1972 SUPER BOWL VI

DALLAS COWBOYS over **MIAMI DOLPHINS** 24-3

Super Bowl VI is played on January 16, 1972, at Tulane Stadium in New Orleans to decide the National Football League (NFL) champions for the 1971 season. The American Football Conference (AFC) champion Miami Dolphins go up against the National Football Conference (NFC) champion Dallas Cowboys.

On an unseasonably cold game day (39 °F) the Cowboys overpower Miami to win their first Super Bowl. **Duane Thomas** rushes for 95 yards and **Roger Staubach** throws touchdown passes to **Lance Alworth** and **Mike Ditka**.

Super Bowl VI MVP: **Roger Staubach**, Quarterback, Dallas

1971 NFL ROOKIE OF THE YEAR

Offense - *JOHN BROCKINGTON*, RB, Green Bay Packers
Defense - *ISAIH ROBINSON*, LB, Los Angeles Rams

1971 MOST VALUABLE PLAYER

NFC - *ALAN PAGE*, DT, Minnesota Vikings
AFC - *BOB GRIESE*, QB, Miami Dolphins

BALL

*Dolphins fullback **Larry Csonka** evades Redskins Linebacker **Chris Hanburger** in Super Bowl VII.*

SUPER BOWL VII

1973 SUPER BOWL VII

MIAMI DOLPHINS over WASHINGTON REDSKINS 14-7

Super Bowl VII takes place on **January 14, 1973**, at Los Angeles Memorial Coliseum in Los Angeles to decide the **National Football League (NFL) champions for the 1972 season.** The American Football Conference (AFC) champion Miami Dolphins face the National Football Conference (NFC) champion Washington Redskins.

Boasting an undefeated 14-0 regular season and despite being shut out in the second half of a low-scoring game, the Dolphins stave off the Redskins for victory in their second Super Bowl appearance.

Super Bowl VII MVP: **Jake Scott**, Safety, Miami

1972 NFL ROOKIE OF THE YEAR

Offense - *FRANCO HARRIS*, RB, Pittsburgh Steelers
Defense - *WILLIE BUCHANON*, CB, Gree Bay Packers

1972 MOST VALUABLE PLAYER

LARRY BROWN, RB, Washington Redskins

He may not break any records, but he won't break any bats, either.

Bats made of Reynolds Aluminum are the best news softball and Little League treasurers (and batters) have had in years. These handsome, beautifully-balanced bats won't break, crack or splinter. They have a "feel" batters like—and they'll take years of slugging. Available in in-the-metal anodized colors, aluminum bats are approved for Little League, American Softball Assn., and U.S. Slow Pitch Softball Assn. play.

In two big NFL rule changes, if a receiver goes out of bounds, either accidentally or forced out, and returns to touch or catch the pass in bounds, the penalty is a loss of down. And If a punt or missed field goal crosses the receivers' goal line, the receiving team may advance the ball into the field of play.

Los Angeles Rams owners Robert Irsay and Willard Keland transfer ownership to Carroll Rosenbloom in exchange for ownership of the Baltimore Colts.

HEISMAN TROPHY

Johnny Rodgers, **Nebraska**, Wide Receiver

NATIONAL COLLEGE FOOTBALL CHAMPION

USC Trojans

ROSE BOWL

Stanford over **Michigan**, 13 - 12
MVP *Don Bunce*, **Stanford**, Quarterback

BASKETBALL

Los Angeles Lakers over New York Knicks
4 games to 1

FINALS **MVP**

Wilt Chamberlain
Los Angeles Lakers

In a rematch of the 1970 NBA Finals which saw the Knicks win in seven games, the Lakers earn their first NBA championship since the franchise moved to Los Angeles from Minneapolis. Led by **Wilt Chamberlain**, guards **Gail Goodrich** and **Jerry West** provide a fierce scoring offense, demonstrating why the Lakers set an NBA record with **69** regular-season wins.

The Lakers (back row l-r) Asst. Coach KC Jones, Gail Goodrich, Jim Cleamont, Pat Riley, Jim McMillian, Jerry West, Flynn Robinson, Trainer Frank O'Neil; (front row l-r) Keith Erickson, Happy Hairston, LeRoy Ellis, Coach Bill Sharman, Jack Kent Cooke, GM Fred Schaus, Wilt Chamberlain, John Trapp, Elgin Baylor.

NBA SCORING LEADER (Season)

KAREEM ABDUL-JABBAR,
Milwaukee Bucks 2,822

NBA FIELD GOAL PERCENTAGE (season)

Wilt Chamberlain,
Los Angeles Lakers, .649

NBA FIELD GOALS
(points per game avg.)

KAREEM ABDUL-JABBAR,
Milwaukee Bucks, 34.8

NBA REBOUNDS
(Season)

WILT CHAMBERLAIN
LA Lakers,
1572 (19.2 avg.)

ROOKIE OF THE YEAR
SIDNEY WICKS
Portland Trail Blazers

COACH OF THE YEAR
BILL SHARMAN
Los Angeles Lakers

UCLA *over* Florida State 81–76

• **Most Outstanding Player** •
**Bill Walton,
UCLA**

UCLA head coach **John Wooden** *— nicknamed the "Wizard of Westwood" — wins ten NCAA national championships in a 12-year period, including a record seven in a row and 5 in the '70s.*

The **22nd NBA All-Star Game** is played at the Forum in Inglewood, CA, with the **West beating the East 112-110.** **Jerry West** of the Los Angeles Lakers is the MVP.

The **San Diego Rockets** relocate to Houston, TX, becoming the **Houston Rockets**, and the **San Francisco Warriors** become the **Golden State Warriors**.

The NBA logo, featuring a silhouette of **Jerry West**, makes its debut.

HOCKEY

art ross trophy
(LEADING SCORER)
Phil Esposito, Boston Bruins 133

calder memorial trophy
(ROOKIE OF THE YEAR)
Ken Dryde, Montreal Canadiens

lady byng memorial trophy
(MOST GENTLEMANLY PLAYER)
Jean Ratelle
Boston Bruins

vezina trophy
(OUTSTANDING GOALIE)
Tony Esposito
Chicago Black Hawks

hart memorial trophy
(MVP)
Bobby Orr
Boston Bruins

horse racing

KENTUCKY DERBY • May 6
Riva Ridge,
ridden by Ron Turcotte

PREAKNESS STAKES • May 20
Bee Bee Bee,
ridden by Eldon Nelson

BELMONT STAKES • June 10
Riva Ridge,
ridden by Ron Turcotte

HORSE OF THE YEAR
Secretariat

MONEY LEADER

JOCKEY
Laffit Pincay, Jr.,
289 wins, 1388 mounts $3,225,827

Riva Ridge & EDDIE SWEAT & Secretariat

Eddie Sweat is **Riva Ridge**'s and **Secretariat**'s favorite guy. Often seen in his plaid or striped pants, Eddie is a groom for the two famous horses. Riva Ridge, the wire-to-wire winner of the Kentucky Derby and the Belmont Stakes is known mostly because he is the stable mate of the great Secretariat. According to the horses' favorite jockey, **Ron Turcotte**, Eddie talked to the horses, forming a very special bond.

Above: Ron Turcotte on Riva Ridge with Eddie in striped pants. Below: Turcotte on Riva Ridge, a wire-to-wire Kentucky Derby winner.

Eddie Sweat with Secretariat and Riva Ridge

Harness Horse of the Year
ALBATROSS

Driver & Trainer, Stanley Dancer with Albatross

golf

U.S. OPEN

Male . . . . **JACK NICKLAUS**
Female . . . . **SUSIE BERNING**

PGA / LPGA

Male . . . . **GARY PLAYER**
Female . . . . . . **KATHY AHEM**

PGA / LPGA LEADING MONEY WINNER

JACK NICKLAUS
$320,542

KATHY WHITWORTH
$65,063

Kathy Whitworth

BRITISH OPEN
LEE TREVINO

MASTERS
JACK NICKLAUS

AMATEUR

U.S. . . . . **VINNY GILES**
British . . . . . **TREVOR HOMER**

Lee Trevino

Gary Player

Susie Berning

Jack Nicklaus

tennis

U.S. OPEN

ILIE NASTASE over **Arthur Ashe**

BILLIE JEAN KING over **Kerry Melville**

WIMBLEDON

STAN SMITH over **Ilie Nastase**

BILLIE JEAN KING over **Evonne Goolagong**

FRENCH OPEN

ANDRÉS GIMENO over **Patrick Proisy**

BILLIE JEAN KING over **Evonne Goolagong**

AUSTRALIAN OPEN

KEN ROSEWALL over **Malcolm Anderson**

VIRGINIA WADE over **Evonne Goolagong**

DAVIS CUP

USA over **Romania, 3-2**

Billie Jean King

Ilie Nastase

BOXING

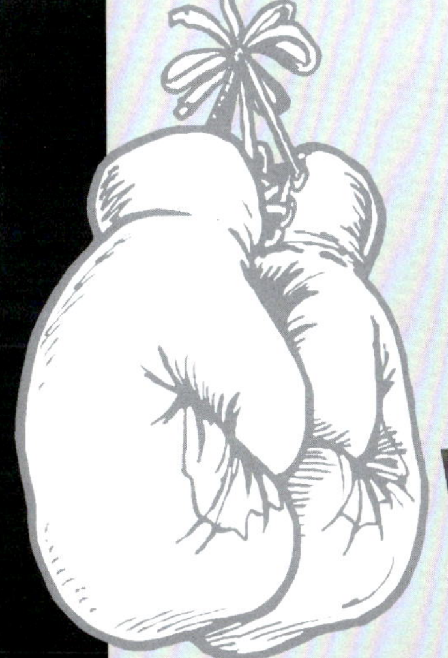

HEAVYWEIGHT
Joe Frazier

LIGHT-HEAVYWEIGHT
Bob Foster

WELTERWEIGHT
Antonio Cervantes

LIGHTWEIGHT
Roberto Durán

Cycling

TOUR de FRANCE
EDDY MERCKX, Belgium
(wins for the fourth straight year)

Boston Marathon
Winner
Olavi Suomalainen
Finland

New York City Marathon
Winner
Robert Karlin USA
Nina Kuscsik USA

BOWLING

BPAA U.S. Open
Don Johnson

PBA National Championship
Johnny Guenther

PBA Player of the Year
Don Johnson

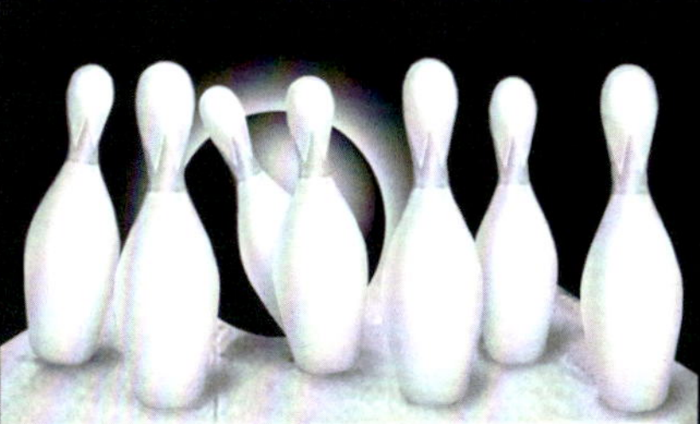

BORN in 1972

DREW BLEDSOE ★ MICHAEL CHANG ★ MIA HAMM ★ DEVON HUGHES ★ DWAYNE JOHNSON ★ KEYSHAWN JOHNSON ★ LISA LESLIE ★ CONCHITA MARTÍNEZ ★ SHAQUILLE O'NEAL ★ DAVE ROBERTS ★ RIVALDO ★ MANNY RAMÍREZ

Shaquille O'Neal

Mia Hamm

DIED in 1972

ROBERTO CLEMENTE, 38 BASEBALL PLAYER ★ GIL HODGES, 47 BASEBALL PLAYER ★ JACKIE ROBINSON, 53 BASEBALL PLAYER

Jackie Robinson

JACKIE ROBINSON was the first African American to play in Major League Baseball in the modern era. He started at first base for the Brooklyn Dodgers in 1947.

ASSORTED AWARDS

JAMES E. SULLIVAN MEMORIAL AWARD

Presented to the most outstanding U.S. amateur athlete

FRANK SHORTER, *running*

ASSOCIATED PRESS (AP) ATHLETE of the YEAR

MARK SPITZ, *swimming*

OLGA KORBUT, *gymnastics*

THE HICKOCK BELT

STEVE CARLTON, *baseball*

Mark Spitz

CHESS

REIGNING WORLD CHESS CHAMPION BOBBY FISCHER, USA

In 1970 and 1971, FISCHER dominated chess to an extent never seen before, leading to his defeat of Boris Spassky to take the 1972 World Chess Championship title.

DOG SHOW

WESTMINSTER KENNEL CLUB Best in Show

Chinoe's Adamant James (2nd year in a row)

Spaniel - Milton E. Prickett, *owner*

BOXING

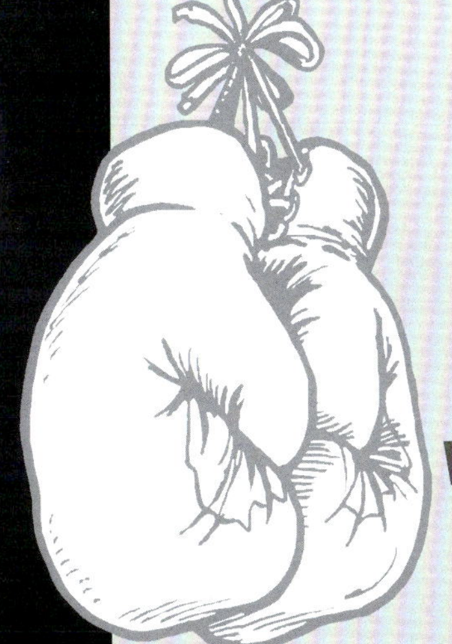

HEAVYWEIGHT
Joe Frazier

LIGHT-HEAVYWEIGHT
Bob Foster

WELTERWEIGHT
Antonio Cervantes

LIGHTWEIGHT
Roberto Durán

Cycling

TOUR de FRANCE
EDDY MERCKX, Belgium
(wins for the fourth straight year)

Boston Marathon
Winner
Olavi Suomalainen
Finland

New York City Marathon
Winner
Robert Karlin USA
Nina Kuscsik USA

BOWLING

BPAA U.S. Open
Don Johnson

PBA National Championship
Johnny Guenther

PBA Player of the Year
Don Johnson

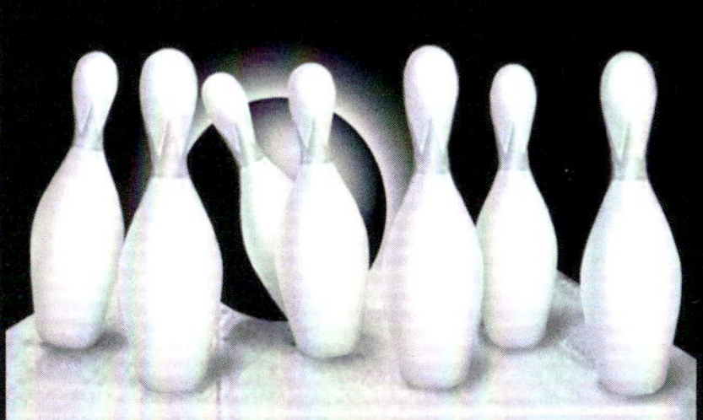

BORN in 1972

DREW BLEDSOE ★ MICHAEL CHANG ★ MIA HAMM ★ DEVON HUGHES ★ DWAYNE JOHNSON ★ KEYSHAWN JOHNSON ★ LISA LESLIE ★ CONCHITA MARTÍNEZ ★ SHAQUILLE O'NEAL ★ DAVE ROBERTS ★ RIVALDO ★ MANNY RAMÍREZ

Shaquille O'Neal

Mia Hamm

DIED in 1972

ROBERTO CLEMENTE, 38 BASEBALL PLAYER ★ GIL HODGES, 47 BASEBALL PLAYER ★ JACKIE ROBINSON, 53 BASEBALL PLAYER

Jackie Robinson

JACKIE ROBINSON was the first African American to play in Major League Baseball in the modern era. He started at first base for the Brooklyn Dodgers in 1947.

ASSORTED AWARDS

JAMES E. SULLIVAN MEMORIAL AWARD

Presented to the most outstanding U.S. amateur athlete

FRANK SHORTER, running

ASSOCIATED PRESS (AP) ATHLETE of the YEAR

MARK SPITZ, swimming

OLGA KORBUT, gymnastics

THE HICKOCK BELT

STEVE CARLTON, baseball

Mark Spitz

CHESS

REIGNING WORLD CHESS CHAMPION BOBBY FISCHER, USA

In 1970 and 1971, FISCHER dominated chess to an extent never seen before, leading to his defeat of Boris Spassky to take the 1972 World Chess Championship title.

DOG SHOW

WESTMINSTER KENNEL CLUB Best in Show

Chinoe's Adamant James (2nd year in a row)

Spaniel - Milton E. Prickett, owner

CAR RACING

INDIANAPOLIS 500
Winner
MARK DONOHUE
162.962 mph avg. in a Penske Racing McLaren–Offenhauser

Jim Nabors sings *Back Home Again in Indiana* during Indy 500 pre-race ceremonies, beginning a 36-year tradition where he performs nearly every year until 2014.

24 Hours of LE MANS
HENRI PESCAROLO & GRAHAM HILL
Equipe Matra MS670

MONACO GRAND PRIX
JEAN-PIERRE BELTOISE

ITALIAN GRAND PRIX
EMERSON FITTIPALDI

NASCAR WINSTON CUP CHAMPION
RICHARD PETTY

Petty

Figure Skating
WORLD CHAMPIONSHIPS

Men - **Ondrej Nepela**
Czechoslovakia
Women - **Trixi Schuba**
Austria
Pairs - **Irina Rodnina & Alexei Ulyanov**
USSR

SKIING

ALPINE SKIING WORLD CUP
MEN'S OVERALL SEASON CHAMPION:
Gustav Thöni, Italy
WOMEN'S OVERALL SEASON CHAMPION:
Annemarie Pröll, Austria

Gustav Thöni

DISC SPORTS

Organized disc sports, in the 1970s, come into their own, beginning with promotional efforts from Wham-O. New tournaments include the Canadian Open Frisbee Championships (1972), Vancouver Open Frisbee Championships (1974), the Octad in New Jersey (1974), the American Flying Disc Open in Rochester, NY (1974), and the World Frisbee Championships in Pasadena, CA (1974).